"A clear, inspiring, and practical ciples needed in our day. I'm grateful for this book and would encourage any Christian to read it, respond to the challenge within it, and step up to live fully as a disciple."

—GAVIN CALVER
CEO, Evangelical Alliance

Tim Sutton is uniquely placed to speak to this core aspect of the Jesus way. He has seen and experienced Jesus followers all over the world and has been able to observe a Jesus way that is effective in all contexts. So much has been written in the subject of discipleship, but Sutton gives us a refreshing new take on this journey. It is well worth the read from an author who lives what he teaches."

—ANDY SIEBERHAGEN
Lead pastor, Heritage Christian Church

"Grounded in a wealth of personal experience and shaped by a wide engagement with Scripture and the wisdom of the Church down the years, Tim Sutton exposes the scandal of discipleship-free Christianity and calls us to walk through the 'Discipleship Gate' into a better way. A great book for getting you started on that journey or as a refresher to get you back on course."

—JOHN RISBRIDGER
Director, Catalyst Leadership and Theology Training Course

"*Think. Pray. Do.* These exercises in each chapter of Tim Sutton's Disciple Gate bridge the gap in much that is written on discipleship between the academic, the devotional, and the practical aspects of being a disciple. Sutton's personal illustrations, wide range of references, and well-structured approach are not only a delight to read, but an invitation to grow through the challenges and trials we face. Practical, pastoral, personal, and highly recommended!"

—RICHARD HARVEY
Associate lecturer in Hebrew Bible and Jewish studies,
All Nations Christian College

Disciple Gate

Disciple Gate

Moving into Life with Jesus

TIM SUTTON

WIPF *&* STOCK · Eugene, Oregon

DISCIPLE GATE
Moving into Life with Jesus

Copyright © 2024 Tim Sutton. All rights reserved. Except for brief quotations in critical publications or reviews, no part of this book may be reproduced in any manner without prior written permission from the publisher. Write: Permissions, Wipf and Stock Publishers, 199 W. 8th Ave., Suite 3, Eugene, OR 97401.

Wipf & Stock
An Imprint of Wipf and Stock Publishers
199 W. 8th Ave., Suite 3
Eugene, OR 97401

www.wipfandstock.com

PAPERBACK ISBN: 979-8-3852-1762-5
HARDCOVER ISBN: 979-8-3852-1763-2
EBOOK ISBN: 979-8-3852-1764-9

VERSION NUMBER 06/21/24

Holy Bible, New International Version®, Anglicized, NIV®. Copyright ©1979, 1984, 2011 by Biblica, Inc.®
Used by permission. All rights reserved worldwide.
Scripture quotations marked MSG are taken from THE MESSAGE, copyright © 1993, 2002, 2018 by Eugene H. Peterson. Used by permission of NavPress. All rights reserved. Represented by Tyndale House Publishers, Inc.
Scripture quotations marked VOICE are taken from The Voice™. Copyright © 2008 by Ecclesia Bible Society. Used by permission. All rights reserved.

Contents

Acknowledgements | vii
Prologue | 1
Introduction | 3

Part I: Beginning
1   To See | 13
2   To Follow | 22

Part II: Becoming
3   Like Jesus | 35
4   New, Whole, and Free | 45

Part III: Being
5   Nourished | 59
6   Grounded | 69
7   Sustainable | 79
8   Mentally Healthy | 90

Part IV: Battling
9   Through Self-Denial and Carrying Your Cross | 101
10   Through Pain and Heartache | 112
11   Through Failure and Slow Growth | 121

Part V: Birthing/Begetting
12   Discipling Disciples | 131

CONTENTS

Conclusion | 148
Epilogue | 151
Appendix: PATHWAYS to Understanding the Bible | 153
Recommended Reading List | 157
Bibliography | 159

Acknowledgements

A SABBATICAL PROVIDED THE opportunity to begin an extended biblical and personal reflection on discipleship. Approaching the waypoints of forty years with Jesus and thirty years in vocational mission and ministry, it was time for both reflection and refocusing. And I had the company of some great and thought-provoking books.

When you have finished reading *Disciple Gate*, I hope that you might continue exploring the theme of discipleship by choosing works from the recommended reading list, which lists those who have inspired me as I have written.

Special thanks to my friend Professor Ian P. Castro for being the first to cast a critical yet sympathetic eye over an early draft of the manuscript. Thanks, too, to Elizabeth Sain for her editorial expertise, detailed eye, and patient heart in helping to check and smooth out the text of this rookie writer.

Any glaring errors or subtle inaccuracies you discover as you read this book are of course mine alone.

Disciple Gate is dedicated to my wife, Annemarij (who has shown me the beauty of sharing life), to my parents, Alfred and Mavis (who have taught me the love and preciousness of Jesus), and to my church family, Westward Ho! Baptist Church, for allowing me to be their pastor over the past seven years—but especially for being the community of disciples and expression of the Body

ACKNOWLEDGEMENTS

of Christ that has most enduringly influenced and shaped my own adventure with Jesus over more decades than I care to mention.

This book is offered with the simple prayer that it will help us to follow Jesus more authentically—starting with myself and the beautiful church community I am privileged to be part of.

Prologue

THE GATE

AN IMPRESSIVE HEDGE STOOD at the bottom of the garden. That's all—at least, that's what they thought. It was dense and overgrown. Many years had passed since much attention had been paid to it.

One day a Gardener was sent to tidy up the hedge and trim it down. And what he uncovered surprised everyone.

As the Gardener cut through years of dense, overgrown foliage and thorny evergreens, his blade struck something more solid. Carefully working, he removed the many layers to finally reveal a small, old wooden Gate.

The Gate opened into a vast and beautiful landscape, rumours of which they had heard for years, told in the legends and fables of the wise.

The townsfolk gathered at the Gate.

Who would dare go through?

—

The hedge is the traditions built up around church.
The Gardener is the Holy Spirit.
The Gate is Jesus.
The vast new land is the place of discipleship.
The townsfolk are us.

PROLOGUE

"I am the gate; whoever enters through me will be kept safe. They will come in and go out, and find pasture."

—JESUS (JOHN 10:9, ALTERNATIVE TEXT FROM NIV FOOTNOTE)

"Enter through the narrow gate. For wide is the gate and broad is the road that leads to destruction, and many enter through it. But small is the gate and narrow the road that leads to life, and only a few find it."

—JESUS (MATT 7:13–14)

Introduction

A GATE IS AN invitation—a portal to new possibilities.

In the Bible, the humble gate is significant. City gates were the places where all the action happened—where important decisions were made, business was transacted, and justice was administered (Deut 25:7; Ruth 4:1; 2 Sam 19:8). Jacob met with God in a dream and declared the place where it happened to be the "gate of heaven" (Gen 28:17). Jesus died for us "outside the city gate" (Heb 13:12). And the Bible closes with a description of the "new Jerusalem." It has twelve gates and, intriguingly, we are told they remain perpetually open to those whose names are written in "the Lamb's book of life" (Rev 21:21–27).

Feel free to continue with your own study of the subject! But this book isn't really about gates. It's about a person who called himself *the* 'Gate' (John 10:9). And it's about following him—in the sense of that John 10 analogy—into salvation life. Another word for this is discipleship.

Discipleship can be a fuzzy, ill-defined thing. "Everyone" (in church) knows what it means but says different things about it if you ask them. We're not always sure who is a disciple and who isn't—or if they even still exist. But discipleship is God's invitation to an epic adventure that will stretch into eternity. The plans, initiative, and power to make it happen are all his, but we have a crucial part to play and moves to make.

INTRODUCTION

Your call is to discipleship—apprenticeship to Jesus—and it will impact every square inch of your existence from the moment you receive him as your Saviour and Lord. It will be a challenging but deeply satisfying and hope-filled life.

Many people falter at the gateway to discipleship and some never get much further. The idea of discipleship is either misunderstood or missing from much of our Christianity. This is scandalous. The suffix "-gate" is of course often added to denote a scandal or controversy. The scandal in this case being that we are neglecting Jesus' self-stated purpose for us. This is contributing to generations of Christians who are increasingly unsure about why they should bother with church—at a time in which the world desperately needs the salt and light that, according to Jesus, is uniquely provided by those who follow him (Matt 5:13–16).

This book aims to help people through the Gate and is also, in a sense, a gate or gateway to discipleship.

Disciple Gate will help us see that discipleship is the normal Christian life and is to be the grand pursuit of the church. It is the way we enter into everything God has planned for us, become who we were born to be, and find the unburdensome life Jesus describes and we long for. And whilst there is a price to pay for authentic discipleship, there is an even higher price to pay for neglecting discipleship. As Dallas Willard says:

> [The] cost of non-discipleship is far greater . . . than the price paid to walk with Jesus, constantly learning from him. Non-discipleship costs abiding peace, a life penetrated throughout by love, faith that sees everything in the light of God's overriding governance for good, hopefulness that stands firm in the most discouraging of circumstances, power to do what is right and withstand the forces of evil. In short, non-discipleship costs you exactly the abundance of life Jesus said he came to bring. (John 10:10)[1]

I feel incredibly blessed to have been able to visit many countries and see the beautiful handiwork of Jesus, building his church.

---

1. Willard, *Great Omission*, 9.

INTRODUCTION

I think of people I've met all over the world—a few of whose stories I'll tell in this book—who have demonstrated that following Jesus is the best way to spend a life: a young Swedish man who showed me what it looked like to live with fire in your heart for Jesus; a Dutch woman whom Jesus rescued from prostitution in Amsterdam, now demonstrating a cleansed and confident life in Christ; a middle-aged South African professor excelling in his career, intelligently following Jesus; an Asian woman willing to give up literally everything to keep Jesus; American teenagers who found joy in choosing to walk with Jesus and going against the flow of their culture; a wise, elderly Kenyan man who sat me down and taught me from Bible and example about living a fruitful life; sharing a room with a Jew and an Arab who both loved Jesus and watching them hold hands each night to pray; friends who have endured sickness, bereavement, relationship breakdowns, mental health issues, and sometimes failure, yet will absolutely not stop following Jesus. For me, the evidence was in long ago: with Jesus we find love, transformation, belonging, and purpose like nothing else on offer.

In the Western world today, there are still lots of churches and plenty of talk about spirituality, but there is not much clarity on discipleship.

We could be part of the biggest and most apparently successful church and yet be missing this essential element. We could be part of the smallest and most outwardly struggling church and yet be in step with the Holy Spirit's plans and purposes. The essential element is discipleship. The urgent need is to understand this and embrace it as individuals and to facilitate the process as churches. Without this we bequeath a weaker church to the next generation—or no church at all. In effect, we drop the baton.

Church leaders can sometimes buy into the prevailing spirit. If we have a reasonable number of people coming on Sundays and good music, we comfort ourselves that things are going well. But something is often missing.

Whilst there are genuine exceptions, discipleship and disciple-making is not usually cited as a success story. In one survey,

INTRODUCTION

60 percent of respondents said their church was not doing well in discipling new believers, only 31 percent set apart time for daily prayer, and only 26 percent felt they had been equipped for sharing their faith.[2] There are excellent groups and organisations out there today trying to rectify the situation.[3] Some are working to see disciple-making "movements."

I believe God has a way for ordinary believers to grow as fruitful disciples that inspires us, feels normal, and is sustainable. I believe that God has already amply provided for this in and through the church, which is the Body of Christ. And we need to understand church for what Jesus called it to be: *a community of disciple-making disciples.*

I often look back to Acts chapter 2 and the inspiring picture it paints of the first church. It clearly describes a gathering of disciples having a great time and watching the church spring up around them. This was a movement energised by people who knew that their purpose was to be and make disciples. Responding to Peter's gospel message, crowds have repented and been baptised. The church grows rapidly, from *120* in Acts 1:15 to *3,120* in Acts 2:41. The writer, Luke, tells us what happened next, in Acts 2:42-47.

> They devoted themselves to the apostles' teaching and to fellowship, to the breaking of bread and to prayer. Everyone was filled with awe at the many wonders and signs performed by the apostles. All the believers were together and had everything in common. They sold property and possessions to give to anyone who had need. Every day they continued to meet together in the temple courts. They broke bread in their homes and ate together with glad and sincere hearts, praising God and enjoying the favour of all the people. And the Lord added to their number daily those who were being saved.

We need a clear, biblical understanding of who we are. There are many valid metaphors for the church: we are the People of God, a Flock, the Bride of Christ, a Building, a Temple, a Priesthood,

---

2. From Evangelical Alliance, *Time for Discipleship?*

3. See the excellent work of Matt Jolley in "What Is a Whole-life Disciple?"

INTRODUCTION

and so on. Each image sheds light on our identity and mission. But we must not lose sight of *the church as a community of disciples.*

Very often commentators refer to this Acts 2:42–47 cameo of the first church and the fourfold devotion of the new believers as "The Four Pillars of the Church." But what if we rather thought of them as "The Four Pillars of Discipleship"? The disciples are devoted to learning and doing the way of Jesus, sharing their life together, celebrating the disciples' meal, and the regular practice of prayer modelled by Jesus to his followers.

The Four Pillars are ways to strengthen, sustain, and empower the community of disciples as they spiritually connect with the One they are following. These first believers thought of themselves as *a community of disciples* rather than *a community of churchgoers.* After all, a community of churchgoers would perhaps only meet once a week. Their aim would be to listen to a message, sing some songs, say some prayers, and go back to their normal lives. They would be more like consumers of religion. A community of disciples, however, might meet more often: for learning, sharing life, worshipping their Master, and drawing close to him. Their focus and attitude would be different. They would be on mission together. They would be an attractive, dynamic group of people to be around.

Many people today are hungry for reality, drawn to community and longing for meaning and purpose. They sense that there is a better way to live in this crazy, crisis-ridden world. We have the answer, and his name is Jesus.

My prayer is that this book will inspire you and help you find what your heart is longing for and what God longs to give you. We discover this in a close relationship with Jesus and in doing life his way, with the community that follows him.

We are at the gateway to discipleship.

Disciple Gate is in five parts, aimed at helping us to explore the calling, goal, power, challenge, and task of discipleship. When I try to explain what discipleship entails, I have found the following five headings helpful:

INTRODUCTION

I. *Beginning:* There is a deliberate setting out on the journey of discipleship, so that we can come to embrace the call of Jesus. The danger is that we never really get going.

II. *Becoming:* We start to understand, focus on, and cooperate with what God is doing to bring about the great goal of our discipleship—to become like Jesus. The danger is that things can stay a bit vague.

III. *Being:* Here is where we learn that following Jesus means being with him in a growing and loving relationship. In the hurry and flurry of these times, this means we are going to need to carefully cultivate new and sustainable rhythms—practices that will help empower our discipleship. The danger is that we never hang around enough to enjoy being in the incomparable presence of Jesus.

IV. *Battling:* Along the way we face some quite difficult moments and seasons. Following Jesus will mean that we make the decision to press on and grow through these challenges. The very real danger is that we give up.

V. *Birthing [or Begetting]:* Maturity, and some would say obedience, requires that we recognise our part in the Great Commission—the reproduction of disciples. As we do so, we help others towards the infinite joys of knowing God and we ourselves grow. The danger is that we neglect this fundamental task.

Following Jesus means much more than trusting in his uniquely atoning death for us. It is more than a vague idea of learning to be "a nice person like Jesus"—which usually associates "nice" with prevailing cultural norms and ignores his harder teachings. It means making the right decisions at key moments as we journey with Jesus.

You can read *Disciple Gate* simply as twelve reflections on key aspects of our discipleship or you can reflect more deeply about the five parts of the book, asking which part speaks the most to you at this point in your life. If you're curious about following

INTRODUCTION

Jesus, if you are excited to start out on your adventure with him, if your journey of discipleship has stalled, or even if you are feeling confident about how you are doing, *Disciple Gate* aims to help you move further into life with Jesus.

At the end of each chapter, there are *Think. Pray. Do.* suggestions for reflection, discussion, and/or action. Having a journal to record your reactions would be a helpful way to engage with what you're about to read.

Come through the Gate and into the land!

PART I

Beginning

I am the light that shines through the cosmos; if you walk with Me, you will thrive in the *nourishing* light that gives life and will not know darkness.

—JOHN 8:12B (VOICE)

CHAPTERS 1 AND 2 look at the first steps we take on the journey of discipleship as we hear and respond to Jesus' *call*.

1

To See

The next day John was there again with two of his disciples. When he saw Jesus passing by, he said, "Look, the Lamb of God!" When the two disciples heard him say this, they followed Jesus. Turning round, Jesus saw them following and asked, "What do you want?" They said, "Rabbi" (which means "Teacher"), "where are you staying?" "Come," he replied, "and you will see." So they went and saw where he was staying, and they spent that day with him. It was about four in the afternoon.

—JOHN 1:35–39

Audient: noun
A hearer; especially, a catechumen in the early Church.

Audient: adjective
Listening, paying attention.[1]

BEFORE I CAME TO faith in Jesus, there was lots of watching.

1. The definitions of "audient" are from www.definitions.net.

Part I: Beginning

Seventeen years of watching my parents, their church, other Christians, the wider world. Listening too—to the Bible being read briefly at the breakfast table; to the Bible stories told by Sunday school teachers; to the tales shared by my missionary parents. I often looked disinterested, appeared antagonistic or amused. But—and I'm as surprised as anyone—it was all going in. Being processed. Claims were being analysed. Lives were being compared and contrasted.

My conviction that God was real and Jesus truly died for me on a cross and rose again didn't appear suddenly, as if from nowhere. It was slowly percolating.

Discipleship starts in a gentle, unthreatening way. Before the invitation to drop everything and join him (recorded in the Synoptic Gospels—Matt 4:18–22; Mark 1:16–20; Luke 5:1–11), John shows us that there was an initial, more informal, period of watching and listening. "Come and see," says Jesus to two men. And it made such an impression on them that they even remembered it happened at 4:00 p.m. (John 1:39)!

This alone is a persuasive example of the power and importance of "come and see"–type ministry. "Come to my house and share a meal with me and my family." "Come, let's walk our dogs together!" "Come to my church quiz night, movie night, exploring faith group." And maybe, after a while of showing them that we truly care about *them* and not simply about filling up our church, we invite them to our Sunday service.

John wants us to read his story and know that, with the first disciples, you and I are also called to come and see. Because to meet Jesus is to meet God himself and find the eternal life he is offering us (John 1:1, 1:14, and 20:31). We are invited to come close, to listen and pay attention.

"Paying attention" is an interesting phrase. And according to scientists it is an accurate description of what it takes for us to deliberately focus on something.[2] We pay. It costs us. It takes some effort. And we're not always good at it—especially our much-lamented, distracted generation. Glued to our smartphones, we

2. Kahneman, *Thinking, Fast and Slow*, 23.

To See

are exposed to a world of information and images yet often blind to the present moment of time and space that we're inhabiting and the real human beings beside us. What hope have we to focus on the Eternal Unseen (2 Cor 4:18)?

Disciples start off their journey by somehow encountering Jesus. How do we begin opening up our lives to him? We could start by recognising the possibility that we are not able to spiritually see as we should. The apostle Paul talks about this in 2 Corinthians 4:4: "The god of this age has blinded the minds of unbelievers, so that they cannot see the light of the gospel that displays the glory of Christ, who is the image of God." In other words, evil prevents people from understanding the Good News that God has come to us in King Jesus, through his cross and resurrection. For Paul, this was personal. For a while it was a literal blinding (Acts 9:1–18), followed by a healing of his sight both physically and spiritually.

Sometimes when I'm giving a talk and I know there are people there who haven't yet started their journey with Jesus, I like to use two illustrations. They are true and well-known stories and, told together, compellingly illustrate some important truths.

The first is the "Invisible Gorilla Experiment."[3] A video is shown to various groups. A game of basketball is played. The instructions are given at the beginning of the clip. Participants are to count the number of passes made by the team in white. After watching the clip, participants are asked if they noticed anything unusual while counting the passes or anything else, anyone else, or a gorilla. Inevitably, at least 58 percent of the participants didn't notice the gorilla. And after rewatching the clip, most of the participants can't believe they missed it the first time.

The second story. World-renowned violinist Joshua Bell played classical masterpieces in a Washington, DC, subway station one morning at rush hour. He played for forty-three minutes. Almost 1,100 people walked by. Only 7 stopped for a while—and only 1 of them recognised him for who he was.

These events show us several things:

---

3. Simons and Chabris, "Selective Attention Test."

Part I: Beginning

1. We can miss out on some extraordinary realities happening right in front of us.

2. Selective focus on one task (like watching the white team pass the ball or getting to work on time) can blind us to other important things that are happening.

3. We are likely to think that the above two points would probably never happen to us.

Maybe we should be more courageous and ask our friends, point blank, if they have ever looked into the extraordinary life and claims of Jesus—and if not, why not. It is more than possible to spend our lives selectively focused on other things and miss out on what is right there for the seeing. Our life experiences, education, and the culture we live in have inevitably taught us to look out for certain things and not for others. We need to doubt the doubts and come with truly open minds and open eyes, not missing the Gorilla in the room, the Virtuoso who is playing for us.

But there is a challenge here also, for those of us already focusing on Jesus. We are reminded that there are always things happening that we haven't yet noticed.

And so let's pause a moment. The best way to read this book is prayerfully.

In keeping with his own experience of coming to spiritually "see" Jesus, it was Paul's passion that others would too. In his letter to the Ephesians, he tells them what he is praying for them (Eph 1:17–19). Taking inspiration from his prayer, we can pray for the same kind of thing for ourselves:

> Dear and glorious God and Father of my Master, Jesus! Thank you for the amazing possibility of moving into life with Jesus! Through your Holy Spirit, please open my heart, my mind, my whole being to let you in. Help me to know you more personally, to see more clearly this life you are calling me into, and to learn to wholeheartedly and perseveringly follow my Lord Jesus—my incomparable Saviour and friend—wherever he leads. And to you be all the glory. Amen!

To See

In the 2022 Edinburgh Festival Fringe, comedian Robin Grainger was looking forward to his show. As he was about to walk in and begin, his technical assistant let him know the bad news. Only one ticket had been sold. Thinking it through, Robin decided to go on stage anyway. He performed his act in front of Mike—whom a reviewer later called his "audient" (as opposed to audience, plural). Mike came out of the show crying with laughter. Unknown to them, the well-known reviewer had been listening at the door and posted on social media the respect she had for a man who would perform for one. This gave an unexpected boost to Robin's career. And Mike became a confirmed fan and friend.[4]

Throughout John's Gospel we see Jesus again and again playing to an audience of one (Nicodemus in chapter 3, the woman at the well in chapter 4, Mary in chapter 19) or just to a couple of men, like in chapter 1.

John shows us that the invitation to discipleship is an invitation to a person and to a relationship. Come and watch. Come and listen.

I'd never heard the word "audient" before and it was interesting to discover the claim that it harks back to early catechumens/disciples of the Christian faith. These were people who learned a body of Christian truth, usually in preparation for baptism or confirmation. Some of us may have done the same and perhaps consider those groups and classes the most focused "discipleship moments" we have experienced.

There have been many periods over the last two thousand years in which various parts of the Christian church have used catechesis to disciple its people. Tim Keller explains:

> This is not the first time the church in the West has lived in such a deeply non-Christian cultural environment. In the first several centuries the church had to form and build new believers from the ground up, teaching them comprehensive new ways to think, feel, and live in every aspect of life. They did this not simply through preaching and lectures, but also through catechesis. Catechesis

4. Jackson, "'One Person Turned Up.'"

was not only for children, but also for adult converts and even for leaders.[5]

The point we are making here is simply that learning the way of Jesus—"new ways to think, feel and live"—is what discipleship is all about. And the good news is that every one of us can and should do that in our own journeys of discipleship.

I'm sure Jesus must have mystified that first small, informal gathering of disciples when he told them that, like Jacob had witnessed so long before (see Gen 28:12), "'You will see greater things.' . . . 'Very truly I tell you, you will see "heaven open, and the angels of God ascending and descending on" the Son of Man'" (John 1:50b–51).

Jacob had seen the angels going up and down a stairway to heaven, but Jesus says that *he* is the stairway—the connection between heaven and earth. (This was a scandalous thing to say. Everyone knew that the Temple was heaven's meeting point on earth.)

Disciples come steadily to see the unique glory and beauty of Jesus and make him the centre of their lives. Over time they may experience a growing sense of the nearness of the Holy One they now belong to. When I look back, I'm amazed at how far he's brought me, but I'm challenged by how far I clearly need to go.

"YOU WILL SEE GREATER THINGS"

I went from avoiding Jesus to wanting him. But we can want for different reasons. At first, I wanted him because of what he could give me—saving me from sin and a lost eternity. Gradually I began learning to love him because of who he is. This can be thought of as the movement from seeing Jesus simply as the *means* of salvation (his death on the cross is what saves me from sin and hell) to seeing him also as the *goal* of salvation, because "all things have been created through him and for him" (Col 1:16). All made *for*

---

5. Keller, "Why Catechesis Now?"

To See

him! That was a mind-blowing revelation to me. Crocodiles and mountains, stars, meerkats, and . . . me. Made for him.

As my focus gradually grew from this merely transactional relationship, where Jesus was simply the means of my salvation, I slowly came to see more of his glory—his beauty. Psalm 27:4 was not yet my reality, but I began wanting it to be. David wants not more possessions or power, but more of God himself:

> One thing I ask from the LORD, this only do I seek: that I may dwell in the house of the LORD all the days of my life, to gaze on the beauty of the LORD and to seek him in his temple.

When we follow Jesus, he opens up a whole new world to us. Life in the Kingdom of Heaven—now, not just when we die! Our understanding—of God, the world, ourselves, and the Gospel itself—expands. And the Bible is the map that keeps it expanding in the right direction.

It is a foundational moment to grasp that we are sinners and need rescuing, that Jesus died for our sins and rose again from the dead, and that we can take hold of this salvation freely through faith in him. But it is not the only important revelation Jesus has for us. God wants, for example, to bring us to understand that Jesus' sacrifice and resurrection is so uniquely significant that not only does it secure *our* personal reconciliation with God and the reordering of our lives but it also sets in motion the restoration of *all reality*:

> For God was pleased to have all his fullness dwell in him, and through him to reconcile to himself *all things*, whether things on earth or things in heaven, by making peace through his blood, shed on the cross. (Col 1:19–20, italics mine.)

The Good News is bigger and better than many of us yet realise.

—

Part I: Beginning

Recently, as our church leadership team met to think about our own journeys of discipleship, my friend and colleague David shared an experience he'd had. As a young Christian, he'd been praying about a certain problem and trying to place it in God's or Jesus' hands. Not yet in possession of a fully-fledged theology of the Trinity, one day he had an epiphany as he was driving along in his car—not too unlike the one Thomas had many years before (John 20:28). He realised that if God could sort it, so could Jesus, because . . . [lightbulb moment.]

David welled up with emotion. As this was in the days before mobile phones, he stopped at the first phone box he found. Phoning his wife, he said, "Rosie . . . just realised . . . Jesus is *God*!!!" As Rosie already knew this, she was quite amused and probably wondered who she'd married. But nevertheless, they are still happily together, and David went on to have a successful career as a chartered surveyor. It doesn't matter who we are, there is much to learn as we walk with Jesus. Some of it may electrify us—at least for a while—and much of it will come as an imperceptible but evolving understanding.

I know I'm still only barely grasping the sheer and unparalleled glory of Jesus. I long to see the Jesus John saw, revealed in his frighteningly resplendent risen and ascended majesty. (Rev 1:10–20). And I'm comforted that Jesus actually wants us to see him as he really is: "Father, I want those you have given me to be with me where I am, and to see my glory, the glory you have given me because you loved me before the creation of the world" (John 17:24).

There is so much more of Jesus to know. So much of his way of life still to learn. He has plenty of "greater things" for us to see and experience. Our casual observing becomes intentional, faithful, joyful watching (read John 20). What an incredibly gracious and patient Teacher he is. Superlatives shed all traces of hyperbole when applied to Jesus.

You and I are invited to imagine a life spent with Jesus. Invited to a relationship with him. Invited to watch him and listen. It's a journey of change and growth that won't leave you as it found you. Seeing leads to other things. Contemplation leads to action. The goal is a changed you, a changed world, and eternal joy (Matt 28:18–20; Acts 1:8; John 17:1–3).

If you are not yet on the road of discipleship, then come along. Expect to have your mind stretched, your heart warmed, and your schedule revised.

In the next chapter, we are going to think about why some people seem strangely happy to believe without following.

THINK. PRAY. DO.

- When did you first get interested in Jesus? What were the key moments in your initial encounters with Jesus and what can you learn from those for helping others to find him, too?
- Looking back at the journey so far, how has your relationship with Jesus changed?
- If you haven't already, commit to practising watching and listening by reading the Gospels, a chapter or more each day over the coming months. Record what you are seeing in your journal.

2

To Follow

"The time has come," he said. "The kingdom of God has come near. Repent and believe the good news!" As Jesus walked beside the Sea of Galilee, he saw Simon and his brother Andrew casting a net into the lake, for they were fishermen. "Come, follow me," Jesus said, "and I will send you out to fish for people." At once they left their nets and followed him.

—MARK 1:15–18

The Jesus way wedded to the Jesus truth brings about the Jesus life. We can't proclaim the Jesus truth but then do it any old way we like. Nor can we follow the Jesus way without speaking the Jesus truth.

—EUGENE PETERSON, *THE JESUS WAY*

ON THAT HISTORIC DAY by the Galilean shoreline, what if *this* happened instead?

TO FOLLOW

"Sorry Jesus. We don't have the time. We have repented from our sins and we believe! We just can't follow right now. But we promise to go to synagogue on Saturday."

The word "follow" is a helpful way of expressing our relationship with Jesus. It communicates a degree of reliance on another. But it is not a passive word. It implies movement, action. Applied to discipleship it infers the process of learning to live like Jesus through thick and thin—"leaving you an example, that you should follow in his steps" (1 Pet 2:21).

We all have a choice as to what or whom we follow. We all follow someone or something—a way of life passed down to us that we take for granted and receive as "the way things are." Christians follow Jesus—but not just in theory.

In first-century Palestine, there were a number of ways on offer. There was, for example, the *scrupulous way* of the Pharisees, the *compromise-with-the-state way* of the Herodians, the *violent revolutionary ways* of the Zealots, and the *reclusive ways* of the Essenes. Each group offered not simply beliefs but ways of life. As there is nothing new under the sun, we can expect these ways to be mirrored in our own times as well. And we should expect that Jesus, likewise, called people not only to a set of beliefs but to a distinct way of life.[1]

As we saw in the last chapter, Simon and some of his friends had spent time observing Jesus (John 1:35–51). And at least some of them had been disciples of John the Baptist. Even so, the way they drop everything to follow Jesus is remarkable. It brings to an end potentially centuries of family tradition.[2] Livelihoods are left behind. Predictability is swapped for uncertainty and sameness for excitement. Something about Jesus made it a decision worth taking. They surely repented, believed . . . and followed.

Disciples are people who have heard the Good News that God is at hand to put everything right. They have responded as instructed—by repenting, believing, and actively, intentionally following Jesus in their daily lives. And when the New Testament

---

1. See Eugene Peterson's *The Jesus Way* for more on the "other ways."

2. See Wright, *Mark for Everyone*, 8–9.

PART I: BEGINNING

refers to disciples, it means both those who *literally* followed Jesus around for three years prior to the cross, resurrection, and Pentecost and those who followed, *figuratively speaking*, in the early church (1 Pet 2:21). Like these latter folk, we too are called to follow Jesus in this figurative but very real sense.

For most of us, faithful discipleship will mean staying in our jobs rather than leaving them. It will mean working out our discipleship in this everyday context, with a whole new focus (Col 3:23). Like the man who wanted to follow Jesus in Mark 5:18–21, following Jesus will, for many, mean that we go home to do that rather than leave home to do it. The level of commitment needed, however, will be the same as shown by Simon, Andrew, James, and John in the account of their calling (Mark 1:14–18).

The word "disciple" is mentioned 208 times in the Gospels and 26 times in the book of Acts.[3] After that it is not mentioned again in the entire New Testament. And this is perhaps one reason we can get confused about who we are today and the life to which we're called. But compare the New Testament's clear preference for the word "disciple" to the scarcity of the word "Christian"—which only appears three times in the whole Bible—and we could naturally be left a bit puzzled as to why the Jesus Movement stuck with this latter term.

We get our word "disciple" from the Latin *discipulus*, meaning "learner, student." But that could conjure up for us a poor reflection of the underlying reality. In Greek the word was *mathetes*. *Mathetai* were people who learned from Greek philosophers or Jewish rabbis. They were apprentices who would follow their teachers around, listen to them, and observe them. They were totally committed to their masters, and their aim was to learn from them and become like them.

We know that Jesus had twelve disciples who followed him everywhere. But he had others too. Luke 6:17 talks about a large crowd of his disciples and Luke 10:1 tells us about seventy (or

---

3. Page 4 of Peter Morden's *The Message of Discipleship* lists Gospel occurrences and I used the search feature on www.biblegateway.com to find occurrences in Acts.

To Follow

seventy-two) others. It is sometimes missed that women as well as men are implicitly and explicitly shown in the Gospels and Acts to be his disciples. As Mary sits at Jesus' feet—to Martha's consternation—she is in essence declaring that she wants to be his disciple and Jesus says that she has chosen well (Luke 10:38–42).[4] Tabitha is referred to as a disciple in Acts 9:36. And, of course, after Jesus rose from the dead and before he ascended to heaven, he gave the commission to make disciples of all nations.

In Acts 11:36 we read about a new label for the young church: "The disciples were called Christians first at Antioch." Did that mean that Christians weren't *mathetai*/apprentices anymore? No. It just meant that the apprentices of Jesus were beginning to be known by different terms ("follower of the Way" is another term that was used, for example—see Acts 24:14). The original meaning of the word "Christian" is thought to be pejorative, since at least two of the three New Testament uses imply an element of shame associated with the term (see Acts 26:28 and 1 Pet 4:16). There were behavioural undertones to the word, related to belonging or being an adherent of. "Christian," then, in no way implies a different type of belief or lifestyle than that of a disciple.

Throughout Acts, the community of believers—those who knew Jesus prior to the cross *and* those who are newly coming to faith post-Pentecost—are often referred to as *disciples* (for example, Acts 6:1, 9:1, 9:26, 9:36, 11:29, 13:52, 16:1, 19:9, 21:4). Though the term "Christian" took hold, the idea that Christians were disciples was never intended to be dropped.

In the book of Acts the original twelve are not referred to as disciples but as apostles (Acts 6:6), presumably to show their different status as well as to avoid giving the impression that only they were true disciples. And, as we'll see in chapter 3, although the words "disciple" or "discipleship" are not used in the rest of the New Testament, the idea and assumption of discipleship underlies and permeates the New Testament letters.

---

4. Bailey, *Jesus Through Middle Eastern Eyes*, 193.

PART I: BEGINNING

So, let's be really clear: A Christian is a disciple. You can't be a Christian and not be a disciple. You can, however, be a disciple that is not pursuing a life of discipleship—to your own and others' great loss!

Repent—have a change of mind, heart, and life; turn to God. You can't follow Jesus if you're walking in the opposite direction! For the first hearers of Jesus' message, as for us, this is an urgent call to break with the past, to turn from sin and godless prevailing cultural norms, aspirations, and agendas and back to God.

Believe—put your confidence in the Good News; specifically, put your trust in Jesus. For that first audience—as for us—the message was an invitation to trust that, in Jesus, God was bringing something wonderful and new. Matthew makes it clear that this new thing is the revelation that God's rule and reign—"the kingdom of heaven" (Matt 4:17)—has come near. And for us, living on this side of the resurrection, believing is likewise not a vague belief that there is a God. It means decisively putting our confidence in the risen Jesus and his achievements for us on the cross (Rom 3:25). As we do, we receive forgiveness of sins and are adopted into his family as children of God (Acts 10:43; Eph 1:5).

Follow—leave behind your old life and learn to do life with Jesus.

In reality—for the first disciples as for us—"repent, believe, follow" is not always a simple, linear process of "1, 2, 3." As we decide to follow Jesus, we never stop trusting him and learning to have *changed minds*, which is what the Greek word for repentance—*metanoia*—means. Repentance and faith are intrinsically part of what it means to follow Jesus. Yet it is a reality that some might think we can follow Jesus without repentance and faith and others may repent and believe but not really set out to follow. I was in this latter category.

In July and August 1986, I was halfway through a two-year catering course, working that summer as a chef in a small seaside restaurant. I was seventeen years old and beginning to sense God gently drawing me towards himself. It was uncomfortable at first. I sensed my life wouldn't stand up too well under his scrutiny. It was also uncomfortable, hot, and pressured in the kitchen and

I was not as gifted as my colleague Martin who went on to be a renowned Michelin Star chef. So, I'd take my cassette tapes along with me to provide a distraction and encouragement. That night one of the secular songs we listened to paraphrased words from Gal 6:7–8: "Do not be deceived: God cannot be mocked. A man reaps what he sows. Whoever sows to please their flesh, from the flesh will reap destruction; whoever sows to please the Spirit, from the Spirit will reap eternal life."

I'd heard those words many times before when I was younger and used to go to church each week with my parents and hear the Bible taught. But tonight, the song was on fire and speaking directly to me. With the kitchen cleaned up and my shift over, I took the ten-minute walk back to our house on the edge of town, went into my bedroom, knelt down on my bed, and said, "God I know you're there. Please will you forgive me, because Jesus died for my sins on the cross. And please, Jesus, would you come into my life." Believing that I was forgiven and determined that my life was somehow going to be different from then on, I climbed into bed and fell asleep.

Whatever that was, it was sincere, it was a change of mind, heart, and direction—it was me placing my trust in Jesus.

Repent and believe? Yes and yes.

Follow? Not quite. Not yet.

Was I at peace with God? My heart said yes.

Was the Holy Spirit now in my life? It's hard to account for the change that began in me from that time, if not for his presence.

Did I clearly know that life was going to be about following Jesus and becoming like him? Yes, and no. I knew something of the language of following Jesus but not so much of what that meant.

Why is that?

There are a whole lot of misconceptions and myths surrounding discipleship.

PART I: BEGINNING

MYTH 1: WE CAN JUST BE ORDINARY CHRISTIANS WHO SIMPLY BELIEVE WITHOUT BECOMING A FOLLOWER OF THE WAY OF JESUS.

I hope we've already dealt with this one. "Disciple" and "Christian" are synonymous. The first twelve were different in that their ministry calling was to be apostles (Luke 6:13). But from the small beginnings of these twelve men sprung a growing community of men and women who followed Jesus and thought of themselves as disciples.

MYTH 2: DISCIPLESHIP IS JUST FOR NEW CHRISTIANS.

Just as Jesus indicated to Peter (see John 21:18–19), the call is to follow Jesus in discipleship for the rest of our lives.

MYTH 3: BECAUSE SALVATION IS BY GRACE ALONE THROUGH FAITH ALONE, THAT'S THE END OF THE MATTER.

I believe there is real confusion here. People think that it's okay to believe in Jesus and remain basically as they are. They are saved, born again, forgiven—going to heaven when they die. What else is there? There is perhaps a vague idea of the need for spiritual growth and change, but not clarity on how that happens and the part we play in the process.

As Dallas Willard once said, "grace is opposed to earning, not to effort."[5] Occasionally we hear the phrase, "Let go and let God." This is good advice for those tempted to anxiously run God's world for him, but it's not the advice Jesus gives people about the kind of life he calls us to. It's more a case of "Let go and follow me."

We have a truly amazing gospel. God has done for us what we could never do for ourselves. The New Testament scrambles for

5. Willard, *Great Omission*, 34.

To Follow

language and metaphors to describe all that has happened to us through Jesus, his cross, and faith in him. We are *reconciled* to God (2 Cor 5:18–19), *justified/declared righteous* in God's sight (Rom 3:24), *redeemed/set free* (Titus 2:14), *forgiven, adopted, victorious* (Eph 1:5–7; 1 Cor 15:57). We live in such amazing grace—grace that is always there, no matter how we feel we are doing. But this grace does not preclude a life of discipleship; it enables it.

And by the way, we don't believe the Good News / gospel and then leave it behind, as if the gospel is the gateway to discipleship but unimportant afterwards. As if discipleship starts by God's grace and keeps going only through our hard work. No. Our discipleship will only be as strong as the grasp we have, in head and heart, of "the glorious riches" of Christ (Col 1:27) that we possess in the gospel. Our discipleship will then be propelled forward as we live securely and gratefully, rather than being guilt-driven, imagining God is frowning on us, or trying desperately to be good enough. It's often been said that we need to preach the gospel to ourselves, every day. If your grip of the Good News is not what it should be, then take some time to study the scriptures on the subject, perhaps with the help of a good book.[6]

MYTH 4: DISCIPLESHIP IS SIMPLY ABOUT ARRIVING AT RIGHT DOCTRINE.

In some of our churches today it can be easy to imagine that discipleship is mainly about right belief, that understanding a set of truths is all that counts. And of course right belief really is important. The New Testament is full of warnings about false teachers and false teaching (as we'll see in chapter 6). Part of our being disciples will be to learn to distinguish the true from the fake. The whole Bible is incredibly important. Too many who consider themselves Christians are trying not just a discipleship-free Christianity but a Bible-free one. Discipleship is, however, about much more than getting our beliefs right.

---

6. I recommend Alister McGrath's *Making Sense of the Cross*, Jerry Bridges' *The Gospel for Real Life*, or John Stott's classic *The Cross of Christ*.

Part I: Beginning

MYTH 5: THE TRULY IMPORTANT SPIRITUAL THINGS HAPPEN MAINLY IN SPECIAL ENCOUNTERS ON SUNDAYS/IN GATHERED WORSHIP.

We point to scriptures that teach us those who "contemplate the Lord's glory, are being transformed into his image with ever-increasing glory" (2 Cor 3:18). Surely all we need to do is fix our eyes on Jesus long enough, through sung worship. Scripture shows us that we surely become like the object of our worship (Ps 115:8).

There is an astonishing truth here. Time consciously spent in his presence is powerful and transformative. Sunday worship can be great—the times when there's a tangible sense of God's Presence as we praise and pray, listen to scripture as it is read and unpacked, or respond by coming forward or taking bread and wine. Occasionally we feel that God has directly met with or spoken to us. We crave such moments. But we are missing out if we imagine this to be the main discipleship event of the week. Sundays are vital for fellowship, learning, worship, and prayer, and for entertaining the presence of the Holy Spirit as a community (Eph 2:22; 1 Cor 14:24–26). Too often Sundays only get our spare change, with other things like sports and family days out getting priority. Sundays and other times we gather for worship, however, are *not* the only important place of spiritual formation.

MYTH 6: IF WE ARE CHRISTIANS AND GO TO CHURCH THEN DISCIPLESHIP IS SURE TO HAPPEN ALONG THE WAY.

Consider the people in the following examples. They are both Christians and therefore disciples. But which one is actively pursuing discipleship?

Olivia goes to church every Sunday. She often feels encouraged by the sung worship and fellowship. Occasionally there is something in the preaching that makes her think. On Communion Sundays, she sometimes finds it helpful to take the bread and

wine and remember that Jesus died for her sins on the cross. The weekly rhythm reminds her of what's important. Olivia loves her church. Then it's back to real life on Monday.

Emma goes to church every Sunday. She isn't a big fan of some of the songs and hymns that are sung (or of singing in general)—but she sings anyway and knows that sung worship at its best can help her keep Jesus central in her life. During the Bible readings and preaching she is listening and alert to anything God is wanting to teach her, that will help in her relationship with Jesus and others, her work, and her witness. She loves to take Communion because she knows it strengthens her walk with Jesus. She feels the regular Sunday worship, fellowship, and teaching helps her to go out and be more like Jesus during the week—so she can hopefully, in some small way, make a difference and influence others to follow Jesus too. Emma loves her church.

Olivia and Emma are both disciples, loved by God and precious to him. There are good things in both examples. They both love church and attend regularly. But the differences are subtle and real. Emma clearly sees herself as a disciple and is more actively seeking to follow Jesus. She is trying to wholeheartedly follow him in the whole of life, as well as to help others to know him. On the other hand, it appears that Olivia's faith revolves around churchgoing rather than following Jesus.

We can't assume that our discipleship will happen without having to pay attention to it. Discipleship is too important to be left to chance and it requires a focus that takes us beyond regular Sunday worship.

MYTH 7: DISCIPLESHIP IS TOO HARD FOR NORMAL PEOPLE.

Some people may feel that discipleship is too costly. We see an example of this in the man we usually call "the rich young ruler": "Jesus answered, 'If you want to be perfect, go, sell your possessions and give to the poor, and you will have treasure in heaven.

PART I: BEGINNING

Then come, follow me.' When the young man heard this, he went away sad, because he had great wealth" (Matt 19:21–22).

Not everyone will be called by Jesus to give up all their wealth. But we all have things that threaten to get in the way of our following Jesus and will need to go (Luke 14:33). So, yes, discipleship *is* costly. But it is not *too* costly. We stand to gain far more than we think we will lose, and to lose far more by neglecting the life God has planned for us.

Some of us have believed in Jesus, but for various reasons we are not truly following him. There is a real tension here and hearts must be searched to see why this is. The call of Jesus to you and to me is to repent, to believe, and to *follow*.

Have you said, "Yes Jesus. I will follow," and started out behind him?

If so, well done! If not, there's no time like the present.

After we have decided to follow Jesus, what comes next?

THINK. PRAY. DO.

- Describe where you stand in relation to repentance, believing, and following.

- Have you ever believed any of the seven myths? If so, which one(s)?

- If you haven't done so before, get alone with Jesus in prayer. Commit to actively and intentionally following him for the rest of your life. Record the prayer and decision in your journal.

PART II

Becoming

The student is not above the teacher, but everyone who is fully trained will be like their teacher.

—LUKE 6:40

CHAPTERS 3 AND 4 introduce us to the *goal* of discipleship, which is to become like Jesus and let him transform us.

3

Like Jesus

My dear children, for whom I am again in the pains of childbirth until Christ is formed in you...

—GAL 4:19

"Putting on Christ"... is not one among many jobs a Christian has to do; and it is not a sort of special exercise for the top class. It is the whole of Christianity. Christianity offers nothing else at all.

—C. S. LEWIS, *MERE CHRISTIANITY*

THE CHRISTIAN FAITH IS, like it sounds, Christocentric. It worships a triune God, yet unashamedly focuses in on Jesus. We could go to all sorts of places to justify this habit, but Philippians 2:9–11 will do just fine: "God exalted him to the highest place and gave him the name that is above every name, that at the name of Jesus every knee should bow, in heaven and on earth and under the earth, and every tongue acknowledge that Jesus Christ is Lord, to

PART II: BECOMING

the glory of God the Father." This focus on Jesus leads us to both worship *and* imitate him, with the goal of becoming like him.

—

I've just finished reading Kazuo Ishiguro's best-selling novel *Klara and the Sun*. It is set in the not-too-distant future and tells the story of a robot. The story follows Klara, an "Artificial Friend" (or "AF") that becomes part of a family.

Spoiler alert: Josie, the young girl in the family, is dying and there is talk of whether Klara might be able to undergo some external and internal adaptations and become a substitute "Josie" when the dreaded loss eventually happens. Josie's dad asks Klara if she thinks she would be able to become "Josie" and Klara responds: "It won't be easy. But I believe if I continue to observe Josie carefully, it will be within my capabilities."

Josie's dad has more questions: "Then let me ask you something else. Let me ask you this. Do you believe in the human heart? I don't mean simply the organ, obviously. I'm speaking in the poetic sense. The human heart. Do you think there's such a thing? Something that makes each of us special and individual? And if we just suppose that there is. Then don't you think, in order to truly learn Josie, you'd have to learn not just her mannerisms but what's deeply inside her? Wouldn't you have to learn her heart?"

Klara answers: "Yes, certainly." Klara goes on to explain that she thinks it would take time, but as humans are not limitless, it must be possible.[1]

Leaving aside any problems we may have with the idea that a human being's spirit might be captured as you might capture information with a USB stick, this is a great illustration of what it means to be a disciple. As Klara would want to "learn Josie," we want to "learn Jesus." And not just act like him externally (which would be quite amazing and revolutionary in and of itself) but to have the same heart he has (which takes things to a whole different level).

1. Ishiguro, *Klara and the Sun*, 242–43.

LIKE JESUS

Happily, this is exactly what Jesus has provided for in the gift of his Holy Spirit. And it is one reason why Paul portrays himself to the Galatians as "being in the pains of childbirth until Christ is formed in you" (Gal 4:19). In a vivid parturient metaphor, Paul, who had previously helped "give birth" to the church, now feels he has to go through that labour all over again. He is describing the agonising work of helping them grow to Christian maturity (see Col 1:28–29). Maturity for Paul means that, both as individuals and as a church, they would become more like Jesus.

Discipleship and disciple-making is not optional for Christians, but neither should it be seen as obligatory in the sense that we do it because we feel, or are, simply obliged to do so. If our discipleship is genuine, it is rather something organic, flowing from the life of Jesus in us. Anything else will lead to either a legalistic or a floppy faith. What we want to do is to have the heart of Jesus, from which will flow a life like his. Obedience to Jesus is crucial (Matt 28:20), but we can't just think that we can obey his commands and we will have "captured" Jesus. We need more—we need the Holy Spirit's continued formation of our inner being.

John Stott (1921–2011) was one of the greatest influences on the Christian church of the twentieth century and a big influence on me personally. In 2007 he gave a farewell address to the Keswick Convention in which he said: "I want to share with you where my mind has come to rest as I approach the end of my pilgrimage on earth and it is—*God wants His people to become like Christ. Christlikeness is the will of God for the people of God.*"[2]

Jesus once said, "It is enough for students to be like their teachers, and servants like their masters" (Matt 10:25a). There is a sense in which we *are* like Jesus now. Through him and in him we are beloved children of God (John 14:20; 1 John 3:1) and John can even say, "In this world we are like Jesus" (1 John 4:17b).

And we *will be* like Jesus. "We know that when Christ appears, we shall be like him, for we shall see him as he is" (1 John 3:2b; see also Phil 3:12). And "for those God foreknew he also

---

2. Stott, "John Stott's Final Sermon." Italics mine.

PART II: BECOMING

predestined to be conformed to the image of his Son, that he might be the firstborn among many brothers and sisters" (Rom 8:29).

We are also invited to become more like Jesus in the meantime. Outside of the Gospels and Acts we may not find the word "disciple," but we do find guidance on discipleship—which is all about growing into our Christlike identity.

Strangely, for many people spiritual growth isn't always associated with the idea of active discipleship in our everyday lives. What if we saw the following verses for what they are—that is, direction for discipleship?

- "Rather, clothe yourselves with the Lord Jesus Christ, and do not think about how to gratify the desires of the flesh" (Rom 13:14). Learn to be like Jesus in his love and moral purity.

- "Put off your old self. . . . [P]ut on the new self" (Eph 4:22–24). Learn the new, righteous, and holy way of life that is yours now that you belong to Jesus.

- "I want to know Christ . . . becoming like him" (Phil 3:10). Knowing Jesus and becoming like him is the normal Christian life. The death of our self-centred life is key.

- "But grow in the grace and knowledge of our Lord and Saviour Jesus Christ" (2 Pet 3:18). Becoming like Jesus involves growing in how we relate to him and to others.

- "This is how we know we are in him: whoever claims to live in him must live as Jesus did" (1 John 2:5b–6). If we call ourselves Christian, we imply that we are living the Jesus way.

- "His divine power has given us everything we need for a godly life through our knowledge of him who called us by his own glory and goodness . . . so that . . . you may participate in the divine nature. . . . For this very reason, make every effort" (2 Pet 1:3–5a).

These verses are all about knowing Jesus and becoming like him, following his way of life. This is the goal of the followers of Jesus. All of the above are challenging and instructive, but the last verse

LIKE JESUS

here is especially breathtaking. God has not just forgiven our sins but enabled us *to participate in the divine nature*—welcomed into the very family life of God for all eternity, starting now.

Through Jesus' finished work it's all done and complete. "For it is by grace you have been saved, through faith—and this is not from yourselves, it is the gift of God—not by works, so that no one can boast. For we are God's handiwork, created in Christ Jesus to do good works, which God prepared in advance for us to do" (Eph 2:8–10). The grace of salvation and the miracle of faith are all, amazingly, a gift. But that doesn't mean there is nothing for us to do after we have received that gift. We are then called to *make every effort*. And *make every effort* is a phrase that appears at least nine times in the New Testament—spoken by Jesus, Paul, the author of Hebrews, and Peter. Not that we are trying to earn our status as God's children—which is impossible—but that grace results in gratitude. And out of gratitude we run towards all that our new identity means for us. We become doers of the Jesus way of life (Luke 11:28; Jas 1:22–25).

There seem to be many who don't equate their faith in Jesus with a life of apprenticeship to him. Dallas Willard writes of what he calls "vampire Christians," who are basically saying to Jesus, "I'd like a little of your blood please. But I don't care to be your student or have your character. In fact, won't you just excuse me while I get on with life, and I'll see you in heaven."[3]

Ouch!

So how can we change, grow, become more like Jesus?

Willard's suggestion is to pay attention to what he calls a "Golden Triangle"—three essential elements to growth as a disciple. They are golden because they are precious. Let's reflect briefly on each of the three points and play around with the ideas.[4]

---

3. Willard, *Great Omission*, 14.

4. I paraphrase Willard here in the following three points (*Great Omission*, 26–30).

PART II: BECOMING

LEARNING THE HEART OF JESUS THROUGH FAITHFUL ACCEPTANCE OF EVERYDAY PROBLEMS

This is why James can say those otherwise incomprehensible words, "Consider it pure joy, my brothers and sisters, whenever you face trials of many kinds." The explanation being, "because you know that the testing of your faith produces perseverance. Let perseverance finish its work so that you may be mature and complete, not lacking anything" (Jas 1:2–4; see also Rom 5:3–5).

This is why Monday to Saturday is every bit as important for our discipleship as Sunday. We learn to face our everyday problems in the way of Jesus. There is nothing more down to earth and natural to discipleship than walking down the road with the Master, facing ordinary but challenging situations, and allowing them to become powerful life lessons. Sitting down for Bible studies is good and necessary, but so often Jesus teaches his disciples when they are out and about and on the move (for example, Mark 10:13–16; Matt 20:24–28 and 24:1–2; Luke 21:1–4).

As we face various circumstances, we think about what Jesus would say or do in the situation we are in, and we remember that God allows us to go through all sorts of trials as part of our spiritual formation (1 Pet 1:6–7; Heb 12:4–12). We persevere. We unlearn old patterns of living and learn new ways. We grow. In chapter 10 we'll explore more of this more difficult yet crucial aspect of discipleship.

INTERACTING WITH THE HOLY SPIRIT IN AND AROUND US

The Holy Spirit is within us, drawing us to Jesus and giving us the desire and power to be like him (Phil 2:12–13; see also Ezek 36:26).

The Holy Spirit works a Christlikeness deep within us, which we call the Fruit of the Spirit (Gal 5:22–23), and gives us the ability to minister, which we call the Gifts of the Spirit (1 Cor 12).

LIKE JESUS

Maturity requires that we grow in both of these areas, though it is the Fruit which more accurately demonstrates the growth of a disciple.

"Spirit-filled" is a term that for many has come to simply mean "charismatic" and active in the more eye-catching Gifts of the Holy Spirit. So it's always good to remember that the Spirit's remit is a little bigger than that. As we learn to pay attention to his gentle but powerful inner presence, he leads us to think, speak, and act in the ways of Jesus.

Crucially, as we by faith fix our eyes on Jesus, we find that the Holy Spirit is transforming us: "Now the Lord is the Spirit, and where the Spirit of the Lord is, there is freedom. And we all, who with unveiled faces contemplate the Lord's glory, are being transformed into his image with ever-increasing glory, which comes from the Lord, who is the Spirit" (2 Cor 3:17–18). This transformative contemplation will involve gazing long and hard at the glory of Jesus revealed through the cross (2 Cor 4:4). Since a basic analysis shows that almost exactly a third of the four Gospels is about Jesus' final week, we should expect to be paying a comparable amount of attention to this climactic season of Jesus' life and its implications for our discipleship.

SPIRITUAL EXERCISES

In the Gospels we see that some activities were evidently important to the Lord Jesus: prayer, solitude and silence, fasting, and scripture memorisation (he was able to quote scripture at will— but arguably only because he had spent many hours committing it to memory and mulling it over in his carpenter's workshop).

We see Jesus escaping from all distractions to pray and fast so that he can feast on the Presence and Word of his Father (Matt 4:1–4). We see him waking up way before the sun comes up—after a breathlessly busy day—to get time alone in solitude, silence, and prayer (Mark 1:35).

I've never been sporty, but like many I am attempting to incorporate more physical exercise into my weekly routine. Spiritual

PART II: BECOMING

exercise is also necessary. These exercises have often been referred to as spiritual disciplines, which I've never thought is a great term. I'm often not that disciplined, so the word bothers me a bit. Even so, these exercises or habits do take a certain amount of effort and . . . discipline.

There is something about periodically detaching ourselves from food, people, and noise that is necessary and powerful for our spiritual formation and nourishment. It is transformative, it is rewarding and rewarded (see Matt 6), and it enables us to truly live (Matt 4:4).

I find Willard's "Golden Triangle" a helpful way to think about the interplay of ways that we can grow in Christ: learning the heart and way of Jesus by persevering through the struggles of our daily circumstances, by paying attention to the Holy Spirit and leaning on him, and by engaging in good habits that feed our spirits. We can move forward in our own discipleship by paying attention to these three key elements. But there are other angles to consider.

WATCHING OTHER BELIEVERS AND LEARNING FROM THEM

In later chapters, we'll look more at the importance of the wider church family for our own discipleship. So here we will simply note that Paul often told disciples to follow his (and other mature Christians') life example as he followed Jesus (1 Cor 11:1; 2 Thess 3:9; Phil 3:17).

Whenever I think of imitation, I think of the true story of José the handyman. Long ago, in the days before Brazil became a missionary-sending nation itself, he worked for the English missionary in a small village in rural Brazil. José didn't see many foreigners and was quite taken with the missionary—who wore sunglasses whenever he left the house, such was the intensity of the sunshine throughout most of the year. So impressed was José with the missionary that he bought and began to wear his first pair of sunglasses. Not quite aware of the etiquette around sunglasses, José wore them all the time, day and night, outdoors and in.

LIKE JESUS

Whether it is by reading biographies and autobiographies, or by observing the way of those you know personally that are following Jesus, the power of example—for good or ill—is enormous. The Bible urges us to avoid "the way of sinners" (Ps 1:1) and tells us that "the righteous choose their friends carefully" (Prov 12:26). We're called to love, not emulate, everyone (1 Cor 5:9–11). And when we do emulate or imitate, we should do it carefully. We may even be led to ask someone who is a little further down the road with Jesus to personally disciple us.

John Stott brings us back to the heart of it all with a quote from William Temple:

> It's no good giving me a play like Hamlet or King Lear and telling me to write a play like that. Shakespeare could do it; I can't. And it is no good showing me a life like the life of Jesus and telling me to live a life like that. Jesus could do it; I can't. But if the genius of Shakespeare could come and live in me, then I could write plays like his. And if the Spirit of Jesus could come and live in me, then I could live a life like his.[5]

Stott concludes:

> God's purpose is to make us like Christ, and God's way is to fill us with his Holy Spirit.[6]

Our goal is to become like Jesus. We mustn't be daunted or discouraged. God has provided everything we need. The Holy Spirit is his precious gift to us. Our part is to cooperate as thoughtfully and wholeheartedly as we can in this process.

The next chapter will look more at the ways we grow and are transformed.

THINK. PRAY. DO.

- In what ways are you becoming like Jesus?

5. Stott, "John Stott's Final Sermon."
6. Stott, "John Stott's Final Sermon."

PART II: BECOMING

- What or who has helped you grow most of all?

- Take one of the four "angles" discussed in this chapter (discerning a life lesson through perseverance in a "trial," cooperation with the Holy Spirit in and around you, engaging in a spiritual discipline, or imitation/learning from a mature fellow believer)—perhaps the one you are least familiar with. Spend time engaging with this angle and recording in your journal the lessons learned.

4

New, Whole, and Free

Therefore, I urge you, brothers and sisters, in view of God's mercy, to offer your bodies as a living sacrifice, holy and pleasing to God—this is your true and proper worship. Do not conform to the pattern of this world, *but be transformed by the renewing of your mind.*

—ROM 12:1–2A (EMPHASIS ADDED)

When we come to new life in Christ, our bodies and their deformed desire system do not automatically shift to the side of Christ, but continue to oppose him. Occasionally a remarkable change may occur, such as total relief from an addiction. But this is very infrequent, and it is never true that the habits of sin are displaced from our bodily parts and personality by the new birth.

—DALLAS WILLARD, *THE GREAT OMISSION*

WE GET NEW HEARTS. Our spirits come alive. Our minds are transformed. Our bodies start learning to behave differently (Rom

PART II: BECOMING

6:12). Discipleship is about a metamorphosis of every part of us (yes, even our bodies will be totally renewed eventually [1 Cor 15:50–52]). The reality is that we are not totally transformed the moment we come to faith in Christ.

In New Testament terms, discipleship involves the essential work of putting off the old and putting on the new, believing truth in place of lies, and living out our identity as children of light. At this point, discipleship intersects with what we sometimes call sanctification. Sanctification is both the settled reality of all who are united by faith with Christ (1 Pet 1:2) and it is the process by which God works to make us holier—not starchier and perfectionistic, but more like Jesus (1 Thess 4:3, 5:23). Discipleship involves our effort in that process. From a secure and empowered position, we are taught to "be transformed."

In this chapter, we will look at three ways we can experience this transformation, wholeness, and freedom.

PUTTING ON THE NEW NATURE

In Ephesians 4:22–24, the apostle Paul exhorts believers to put off the *old self* and put on the *new self*. In Romans 13:14, he talks about "putting on Christ." In Romans 8, he says that our Spirit-empowered task is to "put to death the misdeeds of the body" and live out our new identities as God's children (Rom 8:1–14).

This putting off the old and putting on the new is not something that is done so that we become what we are not. Read that last sentence again, because it's really important. We are putting on the new so that we live out our new identity as disciples, followers of Jesus and children of God. This is made clear in a passage like Ephesians 5:8: "For you were once darkness, but now you are light in the Lord. Live as children of light."

We do not live differently to *attain* the status of children of light. We live differently because of who we *already are* as children of light. So we leave behind the old ways. And the more we live out our new identity, the more assurance we are likely to experience. That is why living in conscious sin, in particular, makes us feel as

NEW, WHOLE, AND FREE

if we are fakes. The reality is that when we sin, we are acting out of our old, fake, and no longer true identity.

The following was not written from a Christian perspective, as far as I know, but there is a lot of truth in it.

> Every action you take is a vote for the type of person you wish to become. No single instance will transform your beliefs, but as the votes build up, so does the evidence of your new identity. . . . Small habits can make a meaningful difference by providing evidence of a new identity. And if a change is meaningful, it's actually big.[1]

As we saw in the last chapter, it's important to understand that the Holy Spirit living in us is enabling the whole process of transformation. One of the most encouraging passages of scripture in this regard is Ezekiel 36:25–26, in which God explains that he gives new hearts and his Spirit to enable his people to live out his ways. Paul picks this up in Philippians 2:12–13—that as we work out our salvation with fear and trembling, it is actually God himself who is working in us to give us the desire ("to will") and the power ("to act") to do what he is inviting us to do and to become what he is calling us to be.

Another way to think about this is to realise that the Holy Spirit has given us the wonderful gift of a new appetite. As babies are born with an appetite for food/milk, children of God are given an appetite for holiness—both the desire and the power to live out our new identity. And so discipleship does not mean trying hard to be good. It means paying attention to the word of God and the pull of the Holy Spirit. It means dropping the old habits we learned before we started following Jesus and learning to distinguish his ways from the ways of the world.

What does it practically mean to take off the old and put on the new? It means to grow in spiritual and emotional maturity, as we see in Ephesians 4:12–16. Paul talks in that chapter about a "way of life . . . in accordance with the truth that is in Jesus" (Eph

---

1. Clear, *Atomic Habits*, 38.

PART II: BECOMING

4:20–21). This is the way of discipleship. And Paul gives the following examples of living that way:

- Replacing lying speech with truthful speech (Eph 4:25)
- Exchanging an angry spirit for a conciliatory one (Eph 4:26)
- Switching stealing for hard work and generosity to others (Eph 4:28)
- Swapping mindless chatter for wholesome, upbuilding conversation (Eph 4:29)

As we ask the Holy Spirit to transform us, we can be ready to spot any *old* way and, with his help, begin taking small steps to replace it with the *new*. Perhaps, for example, you find yourself criticizing others. You know that this is not loving others as God so graciously loves you. So you decide that the next time criticism is on the tip of your tongue, you will stop it in its tracks. *That's putting off the old.* And with the Spirit's help, who knows—maybe next time you'll be able to go a step further and say something positive and true about the person in question! That's *putting on the new.*

We could look at other examples, such as frequently being upset with people—holding onto grudges or being slow to forgive. These are all indicators of spiritual, and *emotional*, immaturity. They are part of the old life that the Holy Spirit is longing to help us ditch. Why? Because we are new creations in Christ (2 Cor 5:17).

But isn't this all too simplistic? Well, it's simply biblical. It is not easy, but with the Holy Spirit's help, it is possible.

In the book of Jeremiah, we read of the calling of the prophet at a young age. Jeremiah responds the way many of us do—finding it hard to see how we can become all that God wills for us.

> "Alas, Sovereign LORD," I said, "I do not know how to speak; I am too young." But the LORD said to me, "Do not say, 'I am too young.' You must go to everyone I send you to and say whatever I command you. Do not be afraid of them, for I am with you and will rescue you," declares the LORD. (Jer 1:6–8)

NEW, WHOLE, AND FREE

Too young, too old, too poor, too rich, too fat, too thin, too this, too that. . . . Jeremiah needed to let the Lord redefine him. Jeremiah was *who God said he was.* So many of us are not sure who we are and are trying to find ourselves. We look for answers in our ethnicity, sexuality, gender, politics, nationality, or activism. God's answer is that we will find ourselves in who he says we are. After all, he made us.

In the New Testament we find the Lord Jesus renaming Peter and others to underscore their new identity now that they are his. The apostle Paul continues in that vein, often addressing his letters to Christians just like us, *not* "to the miserable sinners at Ephesus, Philippi, or Colossae," but "to the saints—God's holy people."[2]

This highlights that it's not simply the old nature that we need to put off. We need to get used to our *new identity* as God's children. A practical way to reinforce this is by prayerfully dwelling on passages like Ephesians 1 with its cascade of references to all that we have in Jesus, and noting the fact that we can call on the further help of the Holy Spirit in this process of growth and change (Eph 1:17–18). Memorising Bible verses or passages that underline our true status is an even better way to renew our thinking.

Serious contemplation on the achievements of the cross will help our transformation. As we noted in chapter 2, the New Testament writers plunder language for ways to communicate all that Jesus has done for us, using cultural images that drive home the wonder of salvation. They do this not to give us big words and jargon with which to baffle ourselves and others—but to create understanding that facilitates growth in discipleship and fuel for mission. Disciples are learning what it means to live in a loving, reconciled relationship with God (2 Cor 5:18–19), as people set free from enslavement (1 Pet 1:18–19), as those declared, as in a court of law, to be in right standing with God (Rom 3:24), adopted into God's family with the full rights and inheritance that comes from being his children (Eph 1:5; see also 1 John 3:1). Each of these metaphors invites us to come and live in its reality and, as its truth

2. Thanks to my friend Pastor Andy Sieberhagen for making me smile as he made this point.

PART II: BECOMING

soaks into us, will send out us to make disciples who transform society through reconciliation, working for freedom, pursuing God's justice for all, and creating loving families.

The reality is that we are fiercely loved by God: "See what great love the Father has lavished on us, that we should be called children of God! And that is what we are!" (1 John 3:1a; see also Eph 3:14–21). The more we grasp the depth of his love, the more we know of his fullness in our lives, the better able we are to make his love known to others. "We love because he first loved us" (1 John 4:19). At the start of Jesus' public ministry, he was given a fresh revelation of the Father's love for him (Matt 3:16–17). This affirmation would be a vital reference point in his life through all he was to face. And if Jesus needed that, just maybe we do, too. Transformation starts within. It flows from a realisation of our true and new identity in Christ.

BELIEVING TRUTH AND THE HEALING OF EMOTIONAL WOUNDS

Sometimes it is not sin or the old self that needs to be dealt with but issues relating to emotional woundedness. There is often a deep healing that is needed here. We can be wounded spiritually, physically, and emotionally and may experience Christ's healing touch on any or all of those areas.

American pastor Dr Terry Wardle experienced a period of emotional distress that set him on a journey of learning how to receive God's restoring touch deep within him and how to minister deeply into the hearts of others with wounds and traumas.[3]

Wardle says that when we see dysfunctional behaviour—from drug or drink abuse to anger problems—there is some kind of troubling emotion underneath. And underneath that troubling emotion is a false belief of some kind. Dig deeper and you may see that under that false belief is an emotional wound.

---

3. See Wardle, *Strong Winds and Crashing Waves*.

NEW, WHOLE, AND FREE

Very often we try to deal directly at the surface level with our own or someone else's behaviour or emotion, but deep change happens as we pray with others to experience Christ's healing presence at the level of false belief or underlying woundedness. This is part of being transformed by the renewing of our minds (Rom 12:2) where we actively look to receive the grace and truth of Jesus. When we experience this grace and truth, with it can come deep healing and restoration. These moments can take place when we pray alone or with others, or in a time of corporate worship. They can happen when we receive prayer ministry.

In 1 Kings 19, we read the story of the prophet Elijah. He was a great prophet—right up there with Moses (Matt 17:3)—but running on empty, having lived for a considerable time in hiding and under immense pressure. After a death threat, he flees into the wilderness. He is exhausted, burnt out, and not seeing things straight. But he runs to where he hopes to encounter God—to Horeb, where God had appeared to Moses years before (Exod 3:1; Deut 4:10). Twice he repeats his skewed understanding of things— "I am the only one left." It's not true, but it feels all too true to him.

In 1 Kings 18:4, we read that there were one hundred other prophets still in the land. And in 1 Kings 19:18, God says there are actually seven thousand faithful people in the land. And so God lovingly meets with Elijah, feeds and refreshes him, replaces untruths with truth, and reveals the next steps for his journey.

God restores our souls. If we're honest, there's a lot of us to be restored. And there are various reasons for our woundedness. These can be traumatic life events that we experience, our sins and the sins of others, or even the sins and woundedness of past generations that continue to impact us today (Exod 34:7). Tools such as the genogram can help us bring these things before God, find freedom, and grow.[4]

We all go through times of stress or burnout and a good number of us go through even more serious mental health issues (chapter 8 of this book will explore this further). We need to know

---

4. See Scazzero, *Emotionally Healthy Discipleship*, 164–72

PART II: BECOMING

that Christ is with us and in us, to restore, strengthen, and pour out his healing love and care.

In the New Testament, Jesus' restoration of Peter (in John 21:15–22) demonstrates the way the Lord continues to heal wounds. The coal fire on the beach evokes for Peter the terrible memory of the denial next to the coal fire in the courtyard. Having forced the issue, Jesus takes Peter for a walk on the beach that will heal the wound that threatened to render Peter unable to embrace all Jesus had for him. Peter gets back on his feet and leads the church into the crucial first phase of its life post-Pentecost (Acts 2).

As we are attentive to our own woundedness and bring those wounds to Jesus for healing, we are enabled and empowered to help others. Paul's words in 2 Corinthians 1:3–4 come to mind: "Praise be to the God and Father of our Lord Jesus Christ, the Father of compassion and the God of all comfort, who comforts us in all our troubles, so that we can comfort those in any trouble with the comfort we ourselves receive from God."

My mum is a great preacher. I'll never forget one of her messages on the wounds of Jesus. Each point started with the letter "V." Jesus' wounds are *vulnerary*, she said. "Vulnerary" is not a word we use much. But it means something that brings healing. So think of that: Jesus' wounds heal our wounds (Isa 53:5b). How powerful and beautiful.

The healing of emotional wounds can be complex and very often we will need the ministry of trusted and skilled others. A profound yet simple way we can begin to learn more about our own woundedness and bring it to Jesus is something called "body outline prayer." We take a piece of paper and draw the outline of a human body (or download one from the internet). Prayerfully and quietly—and ideally with a godly friend who is praying with us—we take time to ask the Lord if there are lies we have believed or wounds he wants to heal. If anything comes to mind, we write the words down on the part of the body outline that seems most associated with that thought. Next, we return to what we have written down, asking the Lord to let us have his mind on what is there. He may call to mind scriptural promises or speak words to our heart. Sometimes these moments can be extremely powerful—as he heals wounds with his word. We can take the paper and write down the truths God has shown. It can sometimes help to symbolically write them over the lies, or to put a big red cross through the paper, reminding us of the love of God and the price paid for us.

If anything more troubling or persistent remains, then it's time to seek out further pastoral help. We shouldn't try to struggle on alone, nor should we minimise these things as unimportant. I have seen many people helped, and have been helped myself, by the reality of Christ's power to heal emotional wounds. There are many ways he does this. The bottom line is that emotional and spiritual wholeness are deeply related.

FREEDOM FROM THE DARKNESS

Our third reflection on transformation is about how God, through his Spirit, may need to address perhaps more troubling issues. Here is where we recognise that "our struggle is not against flesh and blood, but against the rulers, against the authorities, against the powers of this dark world and against the spiritual forces of evil in the heavenly realms" (Eph 6:12).

Experiencing transformation and freedom sometimes necessitates prayer ministry from godly and mature believers, and perhaps leaders. These sisters and brothers can help us experience deliverance from demonic interference.

A short personal story to illustrate.

At the age of twenty-two, I found myself in De Bron Conference Centre in the Netherlands at a mission recruitment conference. You attended for ten days and decided during that time where in the world you would serve for the next one to two years. I chose the mission ship the MV *Doulos*. But halfway through the conference, I sensed the need to ask for prayer from the mission leaders. Over the last couple of years I had struggled to live out my new life with Jesus. I felt the need to pray about things that I knew had not been right. I had also never prayed with anyone about

PART II: BECOMING

my turbulent teenage years. So a time and place for prayer was arranged for that evening.

I arrived to find not just one leader but three. We drew our chairs together and I opened my heart. We prayed together. During the prayers, one of the leaders, Rod, stopped and said, "Tim, were you ever in a jungle area in Brazil (Rod knew that I had spent part of my childhood in Brazil) where you came across a circle of candles with a spirit offering placed at the centre? Did you approach that circle, stomp on it, and knock over the offering?"

What do you say to a question like that?

The thing is, that's exactly what I had done when I was eleven years old. But I had told no one except my parents. And they had never told anyone else.

Rod continued. He said he believed that the Holy Spirit was revealing this because it was the root of a demonic interference in my life and I needed now to renounce various things.

I can't remember the rest of that prayer time except to say that I confessed, repented, renounced, and cried my eyes out, as years of sin and pain poured out into God's presence and the blood of Jesus covered it all. Looking back, this was the beginning of a new experience of freedom and growth.

> And having disarmed the powers and authorities, he made a public spectacle of them, triumphing over them by the cross (Col 2:15).

Whilst parts of this experience remain a mystery, it taught me the following:

One, that we have a very real enemy, not to be taken lightly.

Two, that sometimes we will need to receive prayer to enable the freedom won at the cross to become ours. Disciples need the community of disciples.

Three, that we have a powerful Friend who is on our side (Ps 124:2; Rom 8:31) and ready to speak into our lives.

And four, that Jesus works in and with us to set us free from sin and Satan, to heal our wounds and empower us to live a new life with him (Col 1:13).

NEW, WHOLE, AND FREE

Our lives are a journey to wholeness. That journey takes time. It will only be complete when we are with him in the new heavens and new earth (2 Pet 3:13). At that point our lives will continue, but in a wonderful way that we cannot now fully comprehend.

One of the first C. S. Lewis books I read after the Narnia series was the fictional *Screwtape Letters*. It's a humorously written story about a serious reality—and full of spiritual insight. A senior demon is writing to his young nephew and advising him on how to go about his work. In one letter he writes, "He [God] really does want to fill the universe with a lot of loathsome little replicas of Himself—creatures whose life, on its miniature scale, will be qualitatively like His own, not because He has absorbed them but because their wills freely conform to His."[5]

Our task, with the gracious and eager help of the Holy Spirit, is to put off the old and put on the new, expose the lies and believe the truth, renounce the darkness and embrace the light. For we are followers of Jesus and children of Light.

In the next chapter, we will look at spiritual nourishment for our discipleship journey—the place where we find the power to follow.

THINK. PRAY. DO.

- Which of the three areas we looked at in this chapter has spoken most to you? And do you need to take any steps to address that?

- If you asked Jesus what he most wanted to do in your life, what do you think he might say?

- Talk and pray through your responses to this chapter with a trusted fellow disciple, mentor, or Christian leader.

5. Lewis, *Screwtape Letters*, 39.

PART III

Being

Then, because so many people were coming and going that they did not even have a chance to eat, he said to them, "Come with me by yourselves to a quiet place and get some rest."

—MARK 6:31

IN CHAPTERS 5 THROUGH 8, we look at ways to slow down and grow up, to sustain our vital and intimate relationship with Jesus—*being* with him on the journey of discipleship.

5

Nourished

I am the vine; you are the branches. If you remain in me and I in you, you will bear much fruit; apart from me you can do nothing. . . . This is to my Father's glory, that you bear much fruit, showing yourselves to be my disciples.

—JOHN 15:5, 15:8

I know that if I can stay inside the songs, they will sing me and this night will not be work but play.

—BONO, *SURRENDER*

PAYING ATTENTION TO JESUS means that we slow down to create space for nurturing our relationship with him.

In John 15:1–17, we find one of the most powerful word pictures of the intimate connection between Jesus and disciples. In this chapter, Jesus is building on the message of Isaiah 5 (and Psalm 80) where God is lamenting that Israel, his Vineyard, has

PART III: BEING

not produced fruit. The mission of Israel was to be God's fruit-bearing vine in the world, showcasing what it looked like for a nation to walk with God (see Exod 19:1–5).

So as Jesus takes up that image, he is doing a number of things. First, he's saying that he is the True Israel—he will fulfil what Israel had failed to fulfil. Second, he's talking about the mission of Israel that would now be fulfilled through the disciples—they would be sent to bear fruit. Third, as they went about this mission, they would need to remain intimately connected to Jesus. And fourth, the connection is to one another as well as to Jesus—he didn't say to individuals, "I am the vine, you are a branch." He said "you [plural] are the branches."

So when Jesus says "Remain in me," what does it mean for us? If we check the various translations, we come up with words like *abide, stay, dwell,* and *remain*. The image is of life-giving sap flowing through a Vine (Jesus) to the branches (us), but only if the branches stay vitally connected. This vital connection is the source of life and fruitfulness.

Jesus was always connected to the Father of course, but he kept things "flowing" throughout his earthly life. He often slipped away in the early hours for solitude and prayer—in Bono's words, for "staying inside the song."

If it was important for Jesus to do this, then how much more so for us. And the way we go about it will be crucial. There are mistakes we can make:

- We can falsely assume that, since Jesus is always with us and in us (John 14:23), there is no need for special times of prayer or intentional dwelling with him. Learning to "practice the presence of God" throughout the day is a beautiful habit we surely want to develop. But, as Jesus demonstrates, focused times of prayer are essential.

- We can be so busy in our lives or minds that we altogether neglect this remaining/abiding/dwelling.

- We can ritualise it so that it becomes just another thing on the religious tick list that "we have to do."

NOURISHED

- We can make it all about technique, glorying in the methods we engage in, as if prayer *in itself* were what it's all about.

As we continue in this chapter, we need to keep front and central that we are not talking about ways to be spiritual but about keeping our relationship with Jesus strong and vital. Slowing down for this is vital for our spiritual nourishment.

Back in the introduction, we noted the cameo of the first church found in Acts 2:42–47. We briefly mentioned how it shows the "Four Pillars" of discipleship. From the outset, we see that this new community did everything it could to keep vitally connected to Jesus. It found that those four ways were crucial.

Since both passages (John 15:1–17 and Acts 2:42–47) are about sustaining an intimate relationship with Jesus, let's take a few moments to bring together the words of Jesus and the experience of the first church.

THE APOSTLE'S TEACHING

Here in John 15:7, Jesus says: "If you remain in me and *my words* remain in you . . ." (emphasis mine). Later on, in John 15:9–11, he says: "As the Father has loved me, so have I loved you. Now remain in my love. If you keep my commands, you will remain in my love, just as I have kept my Father's commands and remain in his love. I have told you this so that my joy may be in you and that your joy may be complete."

This is in keeping with what he has already said to the disciples in John 14:23, that the result of this obedience is that the Father and Son "will come to them and make our home with them."

In Acts 2:42, we read that the believers were devoted to the apostles' teaching. This was the teaching of Jesus, passed on to his apostles and taught by them in the temple courts and no doubt discussed in the believers' homes (Acts 2:42–47). It was Spirit-empowered (John 14:26), Christ-centred, founded on and consistent with the Old Testament scriptures. We read, for example, that an apostle's teaching was subject to the test of biblical faithfulness

PART III: BEING

(Acts 17:11). The apostles' teaching is now embedded in the New Testament and although some of these writings were openly attributed to those who were not apostles, the crucial point is that it was considered to be in line with the apostles' teaching, as given by Jesus himself.

Jesus made it clear that new disciples were not just to *learn* his teachings but to *obey* them (Matt 28:19). And so, as they listened to the apostles and let the message shape their lives, their connection to Jesus would flourish. And as we, too, listen, learn, and obey even when it's difficult, we will find our relationship with God flourishing. There may even be a discernible sense of his presence, as the following example illustrates.

Some years ago in Pakistan, a Muslim lady called Bilquis Shah came to faith in Jesus. Bilquis describes her experience of finding Jesus as living Saviour in her book (with Richard H. Schneider), *I Dared to Call Him Father*. She talks about "living in the glory" and describes how she learned to follow Jesus as the sense of his glory would come or go. If he felt distant, she had the keen sense that she was not keeping in step with him.

It would be easy to dismiss her experiences as all very subjective. We may think she was too feelings orientated and did not yet correctly understand the amazing grace of God, who promises never to leave or forsake us (Heb 13:5). But many of us will know from our own experience that Jesus has gentle ways of leading us and letting us know when we are in step with his Spirit. This is to be expected, since we are not involved in simply believing propositional truths but relating to a Person who is *with* us and *in* us (John 14:17).

THE FELLOWSHIP

Biblical faith is undeniably communal. As we've already seen, what Jesus says is to the disciples as a group. He drives this home in John 15:9–17 with a number of references to the fact that remaining in him will mean sharing life with an active and sacrificial love towards one another.

In Acts 2:42, we read that the disciples were devoted to the fellowship. For them this involved eating together, worshipping and praying together, and sharing resources.

Being part of a loving, caring church and receiving ministry from one another is vital, in the original sense of the word. It is essential to life. We are the Body of Christ and each part needs the rest (1 Cor 12). Sunday worship is an indispensable time in the week for nurture. We need to prevent this from getting crowded out by other things or simply neglected. The idea that "I'm a Christian but I'm not committed to meeting regularly with other believers" would have sounded like nonsense to Jesus and his first followers.

It is in this context that love is learned, practised, and developed—the quality of which will win over a sceptical world: "A new command I give you: love one another. As I have loved you, so you must love one another. By this everyone will know that you are my disciples, if you love one another" (John 13:34–35).

As we will see in chapter 7, close connection with the Body of Christ is indispensable to our progress in discipleship.

THE BREAKING OF BREAD

Jesus does not talk about this in John 15, nor is the practice mentioned at all in John's Gospel. That being the case, many see a reference to the meal in John 6 where Jesus talks about the importance of "eating his body and drinking his blood" (John 6:53). For instance: "Whoever eats my flesh and drinks my blood remains in me, and I in them" (John 6:56).

In Acts 2:42, we read that the disciples were devoted to the breaking of bread. The way that it is described has caused many to think that in those early days it was likely an ordinary meal that included the elements of bread and wine—the disciples' meal, instituted by Jesus at the Last Supper.

Communion/the Lord's Supper/the Eucharist—whatever you like to call it—is a vital way we practise remaining in Jesus. We may come from a tradition that isn't so familiar with associating

PART III: BEING

the taking of Communion with drawing sustenance from Jesus himself—or that even is not happy to interpret John 6 in the light of Communion. But it's hard to avoid the conclusion that the Lord's Supper is life-giving when you read the words of 1 Corinthians 10:16—"Is not the cup of thanksgiving for which we give thanks a participation in the blood of Christ? And is not the bread that we break a participation in the body of Christ?" The words of the Communion service remind us that we are "feeding on him in our hearts by faith." Through sharing together in the bread and wine, we are sustained and strengthened in our relationship with Jesus. We neglect this to our own great loss.

PRAYER

In John 15, Jesus only mentions prayer in passing, linking it to what we could call "obedient faith" (John 15:7) and giving a breathtaking encouragement to ask for whatever we wish.

Prayer is a crucial, unmissable part of life for disciples and for church. In Acts 2:42 we see that this, too, was one of the pillars for the new disciples. And because prayer is a vital and often unexplored way of nurturing our connection to Jesus, we're going to park up here and dwell on it for the rest of the chapter.

Intercessory prayer (praying for people and situations) is an important aspect of our prayer life. A recent study came out that examined five churches in the UK that were experiencing quite remarkable growth through conversions. They found a number of important factors commonly at play in those churches. At the top of the list was that there was "an intensity of prayer and fasting."[1]

We are setting our hearts to beat in rhythm with God's own heart when we pray.

You may know the true story of the pastor in East Germany, back in the 1980s, who was so concerned about his world that he started a weekly prayer meeting for peace. Most weeks only a few people came along. But after seven years of persistence, numbers

1. Harris and Remsberg, *On This Rock*, 15.

grew. One night around eight thousand people crammed into the church building and there were seventy thousand or so out on the streets protesting for peace. Two weeks later the prayer gathering is said to have grown to around three hundred thousand. The protesters marched past the Secret Police headquarters praying.

The wall fell—and I even have a chunk of it, from a visit to Berlin in 1990.

We need to cover everything we do in this kind of prayer. One of the great theologians of the twentieth century, Karl Barth, said that "to clasp the hands in prayer is the beginning of an uprising against the disorder of the world."[2] The reality is that, historically, great spiritual awakenings and incredible societal change have come through prayer.

But prayer is so much more than "asking for things." There is, for example, the prayer of examen, meditative prayer, contemplative prayer, authoritative prayer, and, for some, praying in tongues. Just as you might enjoy sharing time with a friend in different ways—singing, debating, dreaming, laughing, crying, complaining, or sitting in silence—there are many ways to talk and listen to God. We should be more imaginative in this.

The prayer of examen has been a blessing to me over the years. There are various ways to go about this ancient practice. We basically set apart some time and space, either alone or with others. We commit the time into God's hands. We ask for the Holy Spirit's help to look back over the previous twenty-four hours—first to see what we are grateful for. We do that again to look for anything more difficult in our day or our reactions to events or people. We bring that to the Lord in prayer. He may have something to say to us about these things. We conclude our time with thankfulness and commit the coming day or week into his hands.

The Lord's Prayer can also be thought of as the Disciples' Prayer, since Jesus gave it to them in direct response to their request for teaching on how to pray (Luke 11:1–4). Whether using

---

2. Barth, "To clasp the hands," https://bibleportal.com/bible-quote/to-clasp-the-hands-in-prayer-is-the-beginning-of-an-uprising-against-the-disorder-of-the-world.

PART III: BEING

the structure of this prayer for our own personal [inserted] prayers or simply praying it as it is ("When you pray, say . . ." [Luke 11:2]), it is a gift to help us grow in our prayer lives. If we even only take the time to learn from the "God-centredness" of the first part of the prayer, it has power to take us out of our self-obsessed tendencies and into the transforming heart of God.

We notice plenty of prayers recorded throughout the Bible. We can meditate on these and allow them to shape our own. We even have a built-in prayer book in the Bible called the Psalms. I recently spent time on retreat in a monastery which sings through 130 to 140 psalms a week and was told that some monasteries manage to pray, weekly, through the entire psalter. I'm currently praying the psalms in my daily prayers—though at a much slower pace!

Why pray the psalms?

- It's a great way to bring the Bible and prayer together.

- The psalms are the prayer book of God's people.

- They teach us how to pray with emotional honesty.

- They help us to pray for things we otherwise might not pray for.

- They help us enter into the joys and sufferings of others. Even if the psalm is not ringing true to my current situation, it surely is to someone else's.

- Some of the prayers may be seen as prayers of Jesus, and so they teach us more about him and his heart (Ps 22, for example).

As I pray the psalms, I go through the passage, reading it aloud all the way through. I read again silently, pausing to make each part of it—as it relates to me—in some way my own. The parts which don't seem to relate to me I turn into intercessory prayer for others. I am led through the psalm into gratitude, worship, complaint, repentance, and more.

Whichever way we pray, we locate the best time or times of day and dedicate those moments or minutes to actively abiding, dwelling with Jesus as our closest friend.

Honestly, there are times when nothing can stop me from getting on my knees and basking in God's presence. And there are times when it feels almost impossible to put aside my anxious thoughts and frenzied activity and be still in prayer. Or times when I just don't want to pray.

There are also occasions when I have not been able to pray, such as the weeks after my dad died and I was in the early stages of grief. Prayer for me at that time meant simply knowing that I was known and held and loved by God (Ps 139) even through the feeling of spiritual paralysis brought on through grief.

Making space for prayer can be an ongoing battle—but it's one I'm fighting and in which I'm seeing some victories. Most of all, I know that when I am regularly in prayer, my connection with Jesus has a vitality and freshness that shows up in my daily life.

INTO PRAYER

As I write this, I am on holiday in Germany's Black Forest. Here in our rented holiday home, I am sitting down on the balcony, with my coffee, to reflect and to pray. A red kite, strong and graceful, soars high above the wooded valley. Nearby a paraglider calmly circles. Both are enjoying the summer thermals on this beautiful, quiet morning. Then a monster. Ripping into the picture, a fighter jet roars through the sky—important, angry, powerful. Three beings—each enjoying the miracle of aerodynamics.

Feeling contemplative, I recommit to not being the fighter jet, tearing through life. I open my heart to God and feel grateful that I can sit here and be refreshed and strengthened in his presence.

Isn't it amazing that a fresh sense of connection with Jesus is constantly possible? In his wisdom, the Lord Jesus has given us the resources of his words to know and live, his people to share life with, bread and wine, and prayer. We could mention other things that do us good and keep our walk with Jesus fresh, such as reading good Christian books, taking a weekly Sabbath, getting time alone in silence and solitude, and the importance of sleep. All involve slowing down the pace to enjoy *remaining* in Jesus and in a very real way simply being in his empowering company.

We find out what works best for us and make time in our diaries for it. But we also explore new ways of growing our relationship with Jesus—both as an individual and with others. We remember the picture of life in the first church—in Acts 2:42–47—that we have thought about in this chapter. We take note that so much of the spiritual vitality available to us comes as we share life in small groups with others. (How many times has that word come up in this chapter—*vital* or *vitality*?)

How beautiful that Jesus is so keen to be intimately connected to us. We need to be sure to reciprocate, slow down, and give proper attention to the most important and beautiful relationship of our lives. As we do so, we are spiritually nourished. Even a few minutes consciously spent with him have the potential to transform both us and our day. The advice to anyone starting out more intentionally in prayer is start small and grow it from there.

In the next chapter, we will look at another important resource for growth in our discipleship.

THINK. PRAY. DO.

- In what ways do you keep your connection with Jesus fresh?

- What other ways might you want to try or feel that you are missing out on?

- Pick a new way (i.e., one that you have perhaps neglected) of dwelling with Jesus and experiment with it for the next week. Record your reactions and learning points in your journal.

6

Grounded

Keep this Book of the Law always on your lips; meditate on it day and night, so that you may be careful to do everything written in it. Then you will be prosperous and successful.

—Josh 1:8

That person is like a tree planted by streams of water, which yields its fruit in season and whose leaf does not wither—whatever they do prospers.

—Ps 1:3

The biblical way is to tell a story and invite us, "Live into this—this is what it looks like to be human in this God-made and God-ruled world; this is what is involved in becoming and maturing as a human being.". . . We are taken seriously just as we are and given place in his story—for it is, after all, God's story. None of us is the leading character in the story of our lives. God is the larger context and plot in which all our stories find themselves.

—Eugene Peterson, "Living into God's Story"

PART III: BEING

I HAVE JUST DRIVEN home from the bottom of town, along a one-way system, up a hill, turning across a busy road onto another road and somehow ending up at home. It was one of those moments when you suddenly seem to "come to" from a sort of hypnotic state and—not remembering the journey—realise that you have been driving on autopilot, not thinking. My only consolation is that I have known these roads for fifty years and driven them more times than I can remember. I know this place like the back of my hand.

This chapter is about "God's Story"—the Bible. Disciples need to get to know this book like the back of their hand—until much of it is second nature. It will shape, grow, and ground our discipleship.

When Jesus ascended to heaven, he said he was sending his Spirit to them (John 14:16–17), not a book. Yet he undoubtedly made provisions for that book, the New Testament, to be written (John 14:26).

Chris Wright suggests that the reason the earliest Christians were so mission-minded without yet having a completed New Testament or having read the Great Commission was that they "knew the story they were in."[1] They knew the scriptures and where it was all leading—the four "acts" of Creation, Fall, Redemption, New Creation—from Genesis to Revelation. They knew that God created it, we messed it up, Jesus is putting it right, and one day all will be made new. They knew that they were living, like us, in between parts three and four of that story. They were disciples—on a missional adventure to bring people of all nations to follow Jesus and share in the kingdom movement, change the world, and live forever.

A great theologian was famously said to have been asked to sum up his vast work of theology. His answer? *Jesus loves me this I know, for the Bible tells me so.*

Quite simply, the whole Bible underpins our lives and mission as disciples. But a troubling theme is recurring. Within churches that have for many years considered themselves Bible-based, the Bible seems to carry less weight—perhaps a symptom of living in a "post truth" world. How should we think about this?

1. In Wright, *Mission of God's People*, 36.

GROUNDED

The apostle Paul believed in discipling others. He invested in the lives of Luke, Silas, Titus, and Timothy, to name a few. And in the letters of 1 and 2 Timothy we have the record of a man writing to his young disciple. A clear theme in those letters is the place of Christ-centred scriptural truth in the life and ministry of the disciple. Look at some of the things he tells Timothy. I'm going to quote a big chunk of it, to show the importance the apostle evidently placed on these things:

> As I urged you when I went into Macedonia, stay there in Ephesus so that you may command certain people not to teach false doctrines any longer or to devote themselves to myths and endless genealogies. Such things promote controversial speculations rather than advancing God's work—which is by faith. (1 Tim 1:3–4)

> The Spirit clearly says that in later times some will abandon the faith and follow deceiving spirits and things taught by demons. Such teachings come through hypocritical liars, whose consciences have been seared as with a hot iron. (1 Tim 4:1–2)

> Command and teach these things. Don't let anyone look down on you because you are young, but set an example for the believers in speech, in conduct, in love, in faith and in purity. Until I come, devote yourself to the public reading of Scripture, to preaching and to teaching. (1 Tim 4:11–13)

> These are the things you are to teach and insist on. If anyone teaches otherwise and does not agree to the sound instruction of our Lord Jesus Christ and to godly teaching, they are conceited and understand nothing. They have an unhealthy interest in controversies and quarrels. (1 Tim 6:2b–4a)

Other important examples of Paul's advice can be found in 2 Timothy 2:2, 3:14–17, and 4:1–5. So much of Paul's advice to his young disciple was about holding onto truth, avoiding error and controversial speculations (i.e., rabbit trails).

Part III: Being

As we follow Jesus, we are often going to come up against these kinds of errors, either in some of the things we have personally believed prior to coming to faith in Jesus or through subtly unbiblical teaching we've absorbed since we have come to know and follow him. Sometimes we meet error in conversations with others.

Paul is not relaxed about all this. He calls some teachings and beliefs "demonic" (1 Tim 4:1). Error is dangerous not simply to our heads but also to our hearts and lives. It leads us down the wrong kinds of paths and even onto "the broad road that leads to destruction" that Jesus warns of (Matt 7:13).

Some years ago, a roll-on/roll-off passenger ferry set off without closing the bow doors. For a short while everything seemed normal, but then water was flooding the decks. Suddenly the ship capsized, causing a heartbreaking disaster that affected many lives. That devastating incident has long been a picture for me that to live with your life wide open to anything is to ask for trouble. As disciples we have renounced sinful ways (Rom 6:1), which for the New Testament involves moral choices (1 Cor 6:9–11). Morals flow from the things that we have believed. Jesus-centred Bible truth matters.

We live in a cultural climate of religious pluralism and relativism that urges us to hold everything lightly and not to claim too much for our personal beliefs: "You have your truth and I have mine." The motivation behind this is sometimes a good one. This world needs a lot more respect and a lot less religious nastiness. But not everything that glitters is gold. Most of us—Christian or otherwise—believe that there is such a thing as truth and that it is knowable and, upon careful inspection, usually distinguishable from untruth. As disciples, we believe in God's truth (John 17:17).

Paul also wrote to his disciple Titus, who was ministering on the island of Crete. Some years ago, Annemarij and I visited the church that was built in a now-remote part of the island where two thousand years ago Titus was martyred for his faith. Titus was also battling unbiblical teaching. Paul says to Titus:

> But avoid foolish controversies and genealogies and ar-
> guments and quarrels about the law, because these are
> unprofitable and useless. Warn a divisive person once,
> and then warn them a second time. After that, have
> nothing to do with them. You may be sure that such
> people are warped and sinful; they are self-condemned.
> (Titus 3:9–11)

How can we deal with error and disagreements about teaching?

Two short stories:

Sharing a meal with a Muslim friend, he started pressing upon me how wonderful Mohammed was. Feeling a little worked up, I started on at him about how wonderful Jesus is. The conversation became strained and voices were raised. Rightly or wrongly, I felt I had the edge over my friend and was quite pleased with myself. Then I realised the truth of the saying that you could win the argument but lose the person.

The moral of story number one is that it's usually better to listen, love, serve, and be gentle than it is to try to overcome someone in an argument.

The second story is about a conversation with a person who felt strongly that women should not preach or be church leaders. He also felt that this was a core salvation issue. In other words, if you are truly saved, you will hold this view of women in ministry.

I explained that there were certain things that were core gospel issues. But there are lots of other things that are secondary. Mainstream biblical commentators usually agree on this—even if they don't agree on what the core is.

Examples of core gospel issues are that we believe that Jesus died for our sins, that he is the Son of God, and that he is and remains fully God and fully human. An example of a secondary issue is whether or not women can be pastors, elders, or preachers.

There are some beliefs—core gospel beliefs—that we hold with a *closed* hand. We will stand firm on those. There are some beliefs we hold with an *open* hand. We acknowledge that sincere Christians hold different views. We may feel they're sincerely

PART III: BEING

wrong, but open- or closed-handed, we're not going to shun them because of it!

Salvation is not a matter of having a mental grasp of the right kind of theology, in terms of a set of beliefs. It's primarily about believing in a Person—the Lord Jesus Christ. In the words of the apostle Paul, "if you declare with your mouth, 'Jesus is Lord,' and believe in your heart that God raised him from the dead, you will be saved. For it is with your heart that you believe and are justified, and it is with your mouth that you profess your faith and are saved" (Rom 10:9–10). "Declaring with our mouths" demonstrates our willingness to stand up and be counted, whatever the consequences, as someone who trusts in and belongs to Jesus.

We are saved by grace, through faith in Jesus, and consequently not by perfect doctrine (Eph 2:8). Yet living a life consistent with faith in Jesus and these core values is part and parcel of faithful discipleship (Phil 1:27; Jude 3–4).

The moral of story number two is that we should try to get to know and understand the core gospel issues and hold onto them with both hands. Without affirming what the Bible clearly identifies as sin, we aim to be as open-handed as possible with what remains. The world doesn't need spiritual policemen and women. It needs women and men like Jesus, full of both grace and truth (John 1:14).

Here comes the *but*.

But there will be times we need to lovingly, strongly, and clearly contend for gospel truth (see Jude 3–4). As Paul tells Timothy and Titus, there are certain teachings that churches must avoid and forbid, purveyors of error that must be warned.

Simply by way of example, here's a brief sketch of some teachings that we should be aware of as we follow Jesus. I have encountered each of these belief systems in those who are part of churches. The first two are more prominent within the Christian community and the third is one we meet in some who are not yet following Jesus.

How would you answer the following from scripture?

GNOSTICISM/GNOSTIC-TYPE VIEWS

This ancient heresy teaches salvation or personal fulfilment through gnosis—secret knowledge. It sees matter as bad and spirit as good.

Any time we imagine that God only wants us to read the Bible and pray and isn't interested in our jobs Monday to Friday, we are being influenced by a gnostic way of thinking. Any time we imagine heaven to be a misty, dreamy, cloudy place instead of being the place where we will ultimately live, on the new earth with real resurrected bodies, we have moved towards gnostic belief.

DECONSTRUCTION

Some believers set out on a journey of radically rethinking their faith and throwing out previously held beliefs, occasionally to the point of no longer identifying as Christians. This journey can result in a departure from positions held by mainstream Christians for millennia. Proponents may take scripture out of context, make claims based on extra-biblical sources rather than claims drawn from the plain meaning of scripture itself, and move away from the Bible to the teachings of men and women. They, rather than the Bible or the church, become their own authority on what is true and what isn't.

Discipleship really does require some serious thinking about our faith, but it is more about *construction* than deconstruction (Luke 14:28). Jesus didn't come to tear up the scriptures but to fulfil them (Matt 5:17). He validates *all* parts of the Old Testament (the only Bible he knew), claiming that they point to him (Luke 24:44), and he prepared for the writing of the New Testament as was noted above (John 14:26). If the scriptures were so central to Jesus, then they will be to us.

The search for truth is good. But we choose not to be "blown here and there by every wind of teaching" (Eph 4:14). Instead, we remain happily tied to the ground of God's word in the scriptures. Those who reject deconstruction choose to position themselves

PART III: BEING

under the authority of the Bible and/or centuries of agreed church positions rather than put themselves at the mercy of an internet search engine.

Lurking not too far around the corner on Strange Beliefs Street are conspiracy theories, held by those who claim to have "done their own research." To some proponents, these theories seem to carry more weight than the Bible itself. We may agree that the world is messed up and that the powers that be [in the heavenly realms] are in cahoots (Eph 6:12; 1 Cor 2:6–8). But we need to keep calm and follow Jesus.

MANIFESTING AND THE LAW OF ATTRACTION

These strange ideas are gaining traction in recent times. Manifesting is the idea that you can bring something into being through aspirational thoughts. The Law of Attraction is a related idea, that thoughts are a form of energy. Negative thoughts, it is believed, will attract negative outcomes and positive thoughts will attract positive outcomes and various kinds of success. This belief is blossoming in America and becoming more common in the UK, and it can be very attractive. Yet it is a dangerous path to walk down. There is a world of difference between trusting God for the things we need and trying to manipulate God or the universe to get what we want.

There is some similarity here to so-called Christian prosperity teaching.

The Bible is our discipleship handbook. It shows us Jesus, makes us wise for salvation, and equips us for every good work (2 Tim 3:15–17). Every part of it can help us to follow him and become like him. It shows us the bigger picture and the wider story that Jesus, and we all, are part of. For these reasons and so many more, we need to carve out plenty of time to read, read, read, listen to, meditate on, memorise, treasure, discuss, and learn to live out the Jesus way of life that it points to.

We come to the Bible with eyes wide open. We admit that it is sometimes shocking and can be culturally offensive to our sensitive twenty-first-century souls. But soaking ourselves in God's Story, the Bible, will protect us from what some have called a "Stepford God."[2] You may remember the movie *The Stepford Wives*, where men had their partners become beautiful and uncritical robots that did whatever they wanted.

A healthy respect for the Bible will help keep us serving the dazzlingly holy Father of our Lord Jesus Christ rather than a tame and domesticated God of our own making. Paul's advice is sound:

> Let the message of Christ dwell among you richly as you teach and admonish one another with all wisdom through psalms, hymns, and songs from the Spirit, singing to God with gratitude in your hearts. (Col 3:16)

In some churches there is the practice of so-called "soaking in the Spirit" in which worship music is played, the Holy Spirit is welcomed, distractions are put aside, and participants are invited to rest in his presence—remaining attentive to anything he is saying or showing.

Regardless of whether we're comfortable or familiar with that practice, there is no denying that, in our busy world, the idea of slowing down to intentionally be with God is good. A few years ago, our church practised something we called "Gospel Soaking" where we "let the message of Christ dwell in us richly." This was during Lent, and over the weeks we read, listened to, and meditated on all four Gospels.

I think "Scripture Soaking" or "Bible Soaking" should be a thing. Come to think of it, it's been a thing for centuries. The ancient practice of Lectio Divina is worth looking into if you have not already done so. It's not exactly "Bible Soaking," but it's pretty close.[3] This age-old practice follows four steps, helping us *read*, *meditate*, *pray*, and *contemplate* through a scripture passage. Lectio Divina invites a slow, quiet, and intentional savouring of God's word and it gives space for us to respond to God.

2. Tim Keller uses this analogy in *The Reason for God*, pages 113–14.

3. Lectio Divina materials are available in many places. One place to access and download Lectio Divina guides is the Bible Society website: https://www.biblesociety.org.uk/explore-the-bible/lectio-divina/.

PART III: BEING

However we do it, we need to be soaked, drenched, and saturated in scripture.

We love our Bible. It grounds us. It helps us to live and flourish as a disciple and find our place in God's Story.

The next chapter looks at some practical, life-giving ways to sustain a lifetime's journey with Jesus in our normal everyday lives.

THINK. PRAY. DO.

- Do you regularly read through the Bible? What methods do you use for this?

- Have you come across any of the "strange beliefs" mentioned in this chapter? What other teachings do you think are harmful to people's spiritual lives?

- Do you tend to shy away from confronting others about error or are you more likely to be argumentative? Ask Jesus to help you with this.

- See the appendix, which describes PATHWAYS to understanding the Bible. This acronym is a tool I have developed to help people learn how to interpret the Bible. It has a suggested exercise to help us grow in learning how to correctly interpret the scriptures. Try it!

7

Sustainable

By this everyone will know that you are my disciples, if you love one
another.

—JOHN 13:35

The challenges we face in our lives as disciples are formidable; without
community they become impossible.

—MICHAEL J. WILKINS, *FOLLOWING THE MASTER*

DISCIPLESHIP IS FOR THE whole of life. It's not a programme we do
down at church for a few weeks or something we stop doing when
we learn "enough." So we are going to need to discover how to sustain this lifelong focus. This chapter will reflect on some important
tools to help us.

Back in the late 1980s, the actress Maureen Lipman famously
played a grandmother in a British Telecom TV commercial ("Beattie"—see what they did there?), in which she was talking to her

grandson about his exam results. The advert became a favourite to many.

> Grandma Beattie: "You didn't pass anything?"
>
> Grandson Anthony: "Pottery"
>
> Grandma: "Pottery! Very useful. Anthony, people will always need plates. Anything else?"
>
> Anthony: "And sociology"
>
> Grandma: "An ology! He gets an ology and he says he's failed. You get an ology, you're a scientist!"[1]

In this book I'm trying not to mention too many ologies, but, as we think about how disciples grow, it may help here to mention the following two:

The first is pneumatology, which is the theological study of the *Pneuma*, the Holy Spirit.

The second is ecclesiology, which is the theological study of the *ecclesia*, the church.

Before Jesus was crucified, rose from the dead, and ascended into heaven, being his disciple normally meant it was possible to see and hear him and be near him physically. After that time—and especially after Pentecost—this of course changed radically. Following Jesus is now possible for people anywhere. In Ephesians 4:10 we are told that Jesus now fills the whole universe! Yet, amazingly, he is not too busy or important to inhabit the individual lives of his followers through the Holy Spirit.

Through two wonderful realities, then, we can experience Jesus and follow him today.

The first is through his Spirit. The Holy Spirit makes Jesus known and leads us to an awareness of sin, righteousness, and judgement (John 16:8). The Holy Spirit is the one who brings us to embrace Jesus and experience spiritual rebirth, and the one who enables us, from within, to follow him as Lord (John 3:5–8; 1 Cor 12:3). And it's the Holy Spirit who lifts the message of Christ from

---

1. Transcribed from "British Telecom 'Beattie Ology' TV Ad 50 Sec Advert."

SUSTAINABLE

the pages of the Bible, gives us understanding, and helps us to live it (John 14:26; 1 John 2:27).

Although we're focusing on the work of the Spirit here, we need to make an important observation. There is a curious similarity between Ephesians 5:18—6:9 and Colossians 3:16—4:1. In the Ephesians passage, the exhortation is to *be filled with the Spirit*, and in the Colossians passage, to *let the message of Christ dwell among you richly*. The anticipated result of each appeal is virtually identical—Spirit-empowered speaking and living.

The reasonable conclusion is that *both* the message of Christ and the Spirit of Christ are crucial for enabling our discipleship. (The "message of Christ" is understood here as the message of Jesus in the Gospels, read as part of the wider Biblical story—the whole Bible needs to "dwell" in and among us.)[2] The reality is that the message of Christ will not mean much to us without the illumination of the Spirit. People are so often predisposed to focus on *either* word *or* Spirit, but we need to aim for a rich experience of *both*.

In the previous chapter, we looked at the importance of the scriptures, so we're underlining here the necessity of being filled with the Holy Spirit. J. I. Packer once said that "[if you] neglect the Spirit [you] lose your focus on the fellowship with Christ He creates, the renewing of nature that He effects, the assurance and joy that He evokes and the enabling for service that he bestows."[3]

We remember also that the Holy Spirit is sometimes referred to as the Spirit of Christ (Rom 8:9; 1 Pet 1:11). The Spirit is the one who brings Jesus to live in our hearts (Eph 3:16–17a). The Holy Spirit thus enables us to know Jesus and have power to engage in all that discipleship entails. Because of this reality, when we say that we follow Jesus, we are not exaggerating. Each one of us can be *personally* discipled by Jesus as we embrace and respond to his Spirit. Isn't that an awesome thought? But it's only part of the story.

The second reality is that we encounter Jesus today through the community of disciples. The operative term here is "the Body

2. See D. Tidball quote in Morden, *Message of Discipleship*, 98n25.

3. Quoted in Morden, *Message of Discipleship*, 92.

81

PART III: BEING

of Christ." When people encounter the church, they encounter Christ's Body. We see an example of this as the Lord apprehends the famous persecutor of Christians on the road to Damascus and says, "Saul, Saul, why do you persecute [. . .] me?" To engage with the Christian community in any way is—quite mysteriously—to engage with Jesus himself. (See Acts 9:4; Matt 25:40). An implication is that to be discipled by Jesus today, we will need (at least in part) to be discipled by the Body of Christ—the church. So, it is no surprise that the next thing that the risen Jesus does is send Saul for initial discipling at the hands of the disciple Ananias (Acts 9:10–19).

To sum up, *pneumatologically* speaking, we can and must each be discipled by Jesus, through the Holy Spirit. *Ecclesiologically* speaking, for the sake of wholeness, God has so arranged it that we need to be discipled by his people.

Those of us who live in the Western world may feel—as the individualists that we often are—quite comfortable with being discipled by Jesus directly. We may suspect that being discipled by the church is going to be harder work, with more commitment. Dietrich Bonhoeffer makes this point strongly: it can sometimes be "easy" to be accountable to God but harder to be accountable to God through the agency of others.[4] But we *will* need both the help of the Holy Spirit and of our Christian brothers and sisters if we are to progress on the journey of discipleship. Practically, that will mean plenty of time with Jesus in prayer and listening and a commitment to sharing your discipleship journey with others.

—

I discovered Juan Carlos Ortiz's book *Disciple* in my early twenties. I found it challenging and inspiring and I still do in many ways. But rereading his story of a regimented seven-day week discipleship programme in cell groups sounds exhausting at best and alarm bells at worst, as it may for many reading these words.[5] How

4. Bonhoeffer, *Cost of Discipleship*.

5. Ortiz, *Disciple*, 133–35.

do we pursue a discipleship that is truly authentic but at the same time healthy, "normal," and sustainable for everyone? How can we pursue an active and authentic discipleship that takes into account our human frailty, season of life, family situation, personality, and learning styles?

When Annemarij and I lived for some years in a faraway country, we experienced what it means to be learners of a new culture and language. For us—as for many other people that we knew—the learning happened in four main ways.

There were *teaching sessions*, where we were part of a small language class.

There was *homework time*, where we went over the language book and tried to personally understand the grammar.

There was *coaching time*, where we paid local people to sit with us a couple of times a week to practise with them and have them correct us and answer our questions.

And there were *practical experiences*, where we lived for the first few months with a local family, and then in our own home, walked through the bazaars, met people, and received and gave hospitality in our home so that we could speak out our new language.

We would then take our new questions back to coaching time and the cycle rolled on.

As the years passed, and we frequently learned from our funny or embarrassing mistakes, we became more and more fluent. Taken together, these various ways of learning were powerful. It's not surprising, then, that we find Jesus using the same kinds of methods to teach his disciples.

There were *teaching sessions*, when Jesus gave "lessons" to his followers. Perhaps most famously in the Sermon on the Mount: "Now when Jesus saw the crowds, he went up on a mountainside and sat down. His disciples came to him, and he began to teach them (Matt 5:1–2a).

There was *homework time*, when the disciples (and sometimes those not yet following him) went away to work out the "grammar" of God's kingdom. Although this was undoubtedly part of their learning experience, we only get glimpses of it as Jesus sends

Part III: Being

people away to work through his teaching. For example, "But *go and learn* what this means: 'I desire mercy, not sacrifice'" (Matt 9:13a, italics mine). And "But when you pray, *go into your room*, close the door and pray to your Father, who is unseen. Then your Father, who sees what is done in secret, will reward you" (Matt 6:6, italics mine).

There was *coaching time*, when the disciples approached Jesus at various moments and asked him questions. "The disciples came to him and asked, 'Why do you speak to the people in parables?'" (Matt 13:10). It is not difficult to imagine the many times that individual disciples, as well as groups of them, approached Jesus in this way—or, indeed, the times that he sought them out.

And there were *practical experiences*, when disciples were sent to sink or swim (preferably to swim) and try out their new Gospel life and language. For example, "After this the Lord appointed seventy-two others and sent them two by two ahead of him to every town and place where he was about to go" (Luke 10:1).

If we applied these four ways of learning to our own journey of discipleship, it might look like this:

Our *teaching sessions* can be Sundays at church. But, to help make these times more of a discipleship experience for ourselves, we can take a Bible and notebook with us, work out what we think God is teaching us, and make a note of our "implementation intentions"—something we will look at later in this chapter.

We never get to the point where we say "I've learned enough now," because our subject matter happens to be limitless, and his name is Jesus. And we commit to embracing the discipline of regular weekly worship, eschewing cultural tendencies to become *church skivers* (who only attend when they feel like it) or *church surfers* (who regularly attend more than one church and in so doing are often split in their loyalties, managing to avoid the accountability of faithful membership of one local fellowship). Instead, we pray that we can be a blessing to and through our local "warts and all" church, come what may.

Our *homework time* is where we choose the best time for our own daily prayer and Bible reading, silence, solitude, or other disciplines.

Our *coaching time* might be time spent with a follower of Jesus who is, at least in one area of their life, further down the road of discipleship than we are. For many of us, valuable coaching time can be spent in a small group, prayer partnership, or triplet in which we practise mutual discipling of one another—giving and receiving encouragement as we study a passage of scripture, share life, and pray together. We particularly want to be using these times to honestly talk about what Jesus is showing us and how we're truly doing.

Small groups are not always the best for this, as it's hard to be honest and open up unless there are huge amounts of trust and the group is "safe." But whatever the chosen context, we agree together that we will share honestly about our lives as we try to follow Jesus—our failures as much as our successes. And we will meet weekly, bi-weekly, or monthly—whatever is sustainable with the normal everyday lives we lead and the life stage we are in. What is right for a twenty- or thirty-year-old will naturally not work for a seventy- or eighty+-year-old.

For the last few years, I've been in a triplet with two other men. We meet most months to discuss the classic writings of men and women who have followed Jesus through the centuries. A couple of hours with these friends does my soul good. We read a chapter before we meet, share a coffee, discuss, and pray. I inevitably come away both emotionally and spiritually encouraged in my personal discipleship. Find what works and is possible for *you*.

Whatever type of coaching experience we opt for, we will need to work wisely and lovingly to bring in the elements of challenge and accountability that facilitate growth in discipleship. For this reason, the intimacy, informality, and confidentiality that comes more naturally to prayer partnerships or triplets sometimes creates a better space for accountability than small groups do. Or for those who are able to find a mentor or spiritual director, those mentorships are also great ways to learn and grow.

Part III: Being

Small groups have played a key part in Christian life since day one (Acts 2:46). Active numbers vary from church to church, but the churches I have been part of have tended to see anything between 30 and 60 percent of Sunday regulars attending one. The higher the percentage, the greater the potential for healthy discipleship to be pursued in a church.

There are naturally those who are unable to be part of small groups, such as parents of small children, those who are unwell or elderly, or those who for various reasons find groups too hard. There will be people who may even have had bad experiences of small groups. For these reasons, triplets or prayer partnerships will work better for some.

In recent years, increasing numbers of people are adapting to the use of online video communication technology that can facilitate meetings when physical gatherings are difficult. For many people, this will always be second best to meeting in person, but it can work well and is only becoming more normalised as time passes.

Our *practical experiences* are Monday to Saturday out in the world around us. Being a disciple is about learning how to live as Jesus would in the everyday life of our family, workplace, community, leisure time, and relationships. It's where we learn to be like Jesus, show the love of Jesus, and wherever we can, by words and actions, proclaim that the kingdom of heaven is near.

We clearly need fellow travellers and we need a plan. It is no accident that Jesus created a group and groups of disciples and that when he sent them out to practise, he didn't send them alone. So if you want to take your own discipleship seriously, then you need a small group or a triplet or prayer partner. Am I sounding like a stuck record yet?!

We want this lifelong learning to be authentic and sustainable. So we need an ology. We actually need at least two: the pneumatology that reminds us that through the Holy Spirit we have direct access to Jesus as we follow him and the ecclesiology that understands that the Body of Christ is essential on the journey—that admits that we need to be sharing our discipleship with someone else.

SUSTAINABLE

I know my own capacity for self-deception. I am a Westerner and have built-in individualistic tendencies. "I can do this on my own," I think to myself. "Maybe I don't need church or small group—I have my Bible! I have the internet and I can watch a livestream or listen to a podcast whenever I want." Or perhaps I rationalize that "I'm too old now, too busy, too *this*, too *that*."

But Jesus gives me the Spirit and the church.

HABITS

As we pursue a life of following Jesus, we will need some good habits. These can be Sunday gathering habits, prayer habits, small group habits, missional habits, or habits of personal growth and character change. And good habits can be built up. We start small.

One idea that we can make use of is something called "implementation intentions" that James Clear talks about in his excellent book *Atomic Habits*.[6] It's not a Christian book but in my opinion it falls under the Philippians 4:8 designation of "worth thinking about." He has some great ideas for habit-building. He also refers to research showing that when it comes to getting people to start some healthy habits, it is neither the command to do so nor a motivational speech that works as much as it is getting them to write down their intention to do more exercise, stating time and place. An implementation intention.

A practical way to try to love your "annoying" neighbour or to become more prayerful would be to discuss your point of growth with your prayer partner, triplet, or small group, pray about it together, and write down your implementation intention. Then, the next time you meet, talk honestly together about how you have got on.

An implementation intention might go something like this: "I want to love X better, so the next time I see her at work this week (at lunch break in the staff room) I am going to ask how she is doing and offer to help her with any need that arises."

6. Clear, *Atomic Habits*, 69–72.

PART III: BEING

Discipleship was never meant to happen merely in a classroom or in the isolation of trying to do it alone. We need the help of Jesus and others.

Our discipleship is not just another thing we're doing down at church—it's a lifelong relationship with Jesus and we need to find workable ways that bring us life and grace as we fail and succeed.

The quality of the love we have for one another is a key part in showing the world we are disciples. And we can't love each other well without spending time together. Disciples need other disciples for discipleship to be sustainable in the long run. God has provided for this through his Spirit and his church.

Psychologists tell us that in the first two years of a child's life the drive to experience joy in relationships is incredibly powerful. When all goes as it should in a child's developmental life, the foundation of "joy strength" is laid. This is pivotal for being resilient through the challenges of life.

> Having enough joy strength is fundamental to a person's well being. We know that a "joy center" exists in the right orbital prefrontal cortex of the brain. It has executive control over the entire emotional system. When the joy centre has been sufficiently developed, it regulates emotions, pain control and immunity centers; it guides us to act like ourselves; it releases neurotransmitters like dopamine and serotonin.[7]

The wonderful thing about our "joy centre" is that it turns out to be located in the only section of the brain that has the capacity for growth and development *all our lives*. This means that growing into genuinely joyful relationships can be a powerful healing experience.[8]

The next chapter looks at how slowing down to follow Jesus is good for our minds and emotions.

---

7. Friesen et al, *Living from the Heart*, 28.

8. Friesen et al, *Living from the Heart*, 35.

SUSTAINABLE

THINK. PRAY. DO.

- In what ways are you sustaining your discipleship?
- Are you more likely to pursue your personal discipleship alone or with others?
- If you are not part of a small group, triplet, or prayer partnership, take a step towards changing that this week.

8

Mentally Healthy

Come to me, all you who are weary and burdened, and I will give you rest. Take my yoke upon you and learn from me, for I am gentle and humble in heart, and you will find rest for your souls. For my yoke is easy and my burden is light.

—MATT 11:28–30

The unwounded life bears no resemblance to the Rabbi.

—BRENNAN MANNING, *ABBA'S CHILD*

WE ALL WALK WITH a limp. Is discipleship safe?

Maybe the real question is whether Jesus is safe.

Anyone who has experienced mental illness—firsthand or through a loved one—will know that these are not simply academic questions. It is sometimes suggested that "Jesus, religion, or anything like that" can be harmful to mental health.

MENTALLY HEALTHY

Hardly a week passes without new statistics on the increasing numbers of people affected by mental health problems.[1] So it is important to say something here about this issue. Even if we ourselves are not facing questions related to mental health, we are certain to regularly rub shoulders with those who are.

As a pastor I have encountered many people's stories of mental health. But it has also been close to home. Some years ago my lovely wife Annemarij went through some dark times of mental breakdown. Anxiety developed into psychosis. The psychosis returned a number of times. Annemarij was hospitalised for some days and on a second occasion for some weeks. During that intensely disorientating and frightening time, she was unable to distinguish between delusions and reality.

Reflecting on causes and triggers, Annemarij looks back on the painful loss of her mother at the vulnerable age of fourteen—a bereavement that she emotionally shoved away and had not dealt with properly. Delayed grief began to emerge in her late twenties and thirties. This grief was compounded when, at the age of forty and after eleven years of marriage, it became apparent that we could not have children. Workplace pressures and stresses at church were the tipping point.

Over the past eight years the psychosis has not returned. It has been vital for Annemarij, however, to become more self-aware, so that she can spot the warning signs and step back from things when she needs to. Coming to know her own limits in this way and not push too hard against them, medication, work she enjoys, good friends, a loving church community, therapy, and a supportive husband (who still manages to find the time to drive her round the bend) have helped her to this place. But she will tell you that her relationship with God has by necessity changed and she is these days walking more gently and calmly with Jesus—which doesn't come naturally to a passionate heart like hers.

I have never experienced all that Annemarij has had to carry, but after living together through the trauma of her last

---

1. For example, see Milliken, "Depression and Anxiety," which describes post-pandemic rises in depression, anxiety, and other health conditions.

PART III: BEING

hospitalisation, I was signed off work for several weeks with anxiety. An excellent GP prescribed medication to help me sleep. I received counselling and made a phased return to work. Through this I got just a taste of the fragility of mental health and the cost both to those who suffer and to their loved ones. I now advise people with any concerns about their mental health both to visit their GP as a first point of call and to allow other, trusted, people to share the discipleship journey with them.

Jesus' invitation to be his disciple in Matthew 11:28–30 is beautiful. Many of us will be familiar with Eugene Peterson's translation of the passage in *The Message*:

> Are you tired? Worn out? Burned out on religion? Come to me. Get away with me and you'll recover your life. I'll show you how to take a real rest. Walk with me and work with me—watch how I do it. Learn the unforced rhythms of grace. I won't lay anything heavy or ill-fitting on you. Keep company with me and you'll learn to live freely and lightly.

These words bring out the "burnedoutness" that religion can bring—even some types of Bible religion. But they are words that apply equally to any way of doing life that drags us down. The claim of Jesus here is that the way of discipleship—his way—will not drag you down but help bring rest for your soul.

The image here is that of a pair of oxen wearing a shared wooden harness. The younger of the animals is joined with the older and stronger in order to stop him from charging along and ploughing at a pace that is not sustainable and will make him collapse before the end of the day.

The Jewish people spoke of the yoke of the law. But Jesus is talking about the yoke of himself. He is describing a partnership in which he as the senior partner will help us through. There is still work to be done—the burden of life is still there, but it is now a shared burden. Discipleship is a partnership with you and Jesus. You will make it through with his "pulling power."[2]

2. See the Life Application Study Bible, NIV, note on Matthew 11:30: "Jesus doesn't offer a life of luxurious ease—the yoke is still an oxen's tool for working

For these reasons and more, we can say discipleship is safe because Jesus is safe.

But there are things to be aware of, both for disciples who have experienced mental health challenges and for the rest of us, as we walk together.

Mental health problems come in a vast array of ways and generalising is impossible. Those who have struggled or who continue to struggle with mental health may sometimes find the following:

- Feeling nervous about worship services, where it's easy to get caught up in the moment and feel that you're out of control or "losing yourself"

- Anxiety about people's expectations of your presence and involvement in church

- The need for more sleep than others

- Hypersensitivity to insensitive comments and unkind or inconsiderate behaviour

- Feeling judged

- Confusion about hearing God's voice

- Fear when the problems of the world are spoken of

- Perception that Christians think that all illnesses are a sign of lack of faith and should be healed this side of the New Creation

- Poor sense of self-worth

- Difficulty grasping the nuances of self-denial/carrying your cross and following Jesus, whilst at the same time learning to pay attention to your own needs and be kind to yourself

- Difficulty with boundaries in general

Consider the following words from psychiatrist Christopher C. H. Cook, who is also a Christian minister. He writes that "mental

---

hard. But it is a shared yoke, with weight falling on bigger shoulders than yours. Someone with more pulling power is up front helping. Suddenly you are participating in life's responsibilities with a great Partner."

PART III: BEING

health and spiritual wellbeing are inextricably intertwined."[3] In an excellent treatment of Jesus' Sermon on the Mount in Matthew 5–7, Cook explores how so many of the themes we find there are fertile ground for speaking to human wellbeing and flourishing, starting as they do with the teaching that blessed (happy, fortunate, flourishing) are the poor in spirit and those who mourn. A long quote, but helpful:

> As a psychiatrist reading the Sermon on the Mount, I am struck by the great extent of its attention to the same things I have been concerned with in my clinical practice in the past, and in my ongoing academic work in the field of mental health. . . . Jesus probes us . . . about what we really desire, and why we worry about the things that we do, all of which are central to what we would call mental wellbeing. He asks us difficult questions about how we relate to one another, and to God, when we face conflict, failure and human selfishness (our own, or that of others). When Jesus talks about forgiveness he [centres on] . . . the reality of our need for divine help to give and receive forgiveness. Forgiveness has the power to heal us. But it is also something simply beyond human grasp. Prayer is at the heart of the Sermon on the Mount. I would go so far as to suggest that it is at the heart of the therapy that Jesus offers for the human condition.[4]

Our discipleship and disciple-making needs to be countercultural. Bigger and faster is always better in the world we live in. Active, passionate, and driven is the Christianity of many of our evangelical/charismatic churches. "Easy and light" and unburdensome are the marks of the discipleship the Lord Jesus commissions.

Peter Maiden's experience is probably not unique:

> It's amazing how many discipleship challenges have been placed on me over the years. These have often been presented as 'must do' things, in order to be a true disciple. I have been told I must have a quiet time every day. I must read the Bible through every year. I must spend a

3. Cook, "What Did Jesus Have to Say," 138.
4. Cook, "What Did Jesus Have to Say," 137.

minimum of an hour in prayer every day. I must speak
to at least one person about Jesus every day, and the list
continues. The list of things I must not do in order to be
a true disciple is even longer![5]

As Peter Maiden goes on to point out, prayer and Bible and wit-
nessing are all important. But they come from living in a loving relationship with Jesus. Jesus doesn't come to us with a list of dos and
don'ts. He comes with strong but gentle steering into right paths.

If discipleship is about a lifelong journey towards growth,
change, and wholeness, what does that mean for those who suffer long-term mental illness? Change can feel impossible for
anyone, let alone those who travel this particular journey. Well-
meaning people can suggest that we should not "pressure" people
to change—let people know "it's okay not to be okay." Yes. But. We
want people to know that with Jesus there is always hope. And
other well-meaning people can suggest that there is full healing to
be had right now if we only believe, pray, try hard enough.

In their excellent book *Mental Health and Your Church: A
Handbook for Biblical Care*, Helen Thorne and Dr Steve Midgely
make some suggestions. For those of us suffering with mental ill
health and for those of us who want to be of help, they suggest that
we can dream of *complete healing in the long-term*—by which they
mean in the new heavens and new earth (2 Pet 3:13); *thriving in
the medium term*; and *perseverance with hope in the short term*.[6]
Slowly but surely we can learn and help each other learn how to
take off "old self thoughts" and put on the new self (Eph 4:22–24).
They conclude:

> All humans change slowly. Those who are struggling may
> change particularly slowly—they're following their Sav-
> iour with a more pronounced limp than others. But there
> is hope. And once someone begins to change, there is no
> telling how exciting that change might become.[7]

---

5. Maiden, *Discipleship*, 19.

6. Thorne and Midgley, *Mental Health and Your Church*, 108.

7. Thorne and Midgley, *Mental Health and Your Church*, 111.

PART III: BEING

Discipleship is a lifelong journey and it's good to walk slowly. Mentally healthy discipleship will involve learning to be vulnerable with each other as we share lives and are genuinely supportive. It will involve learning how to accept each other as God accepts us. It will involve learning to pray in honest ways and to lament— the biblical way of speaking out our pain to God in the context of prayer and worship (Ps 13, for example). It will involve paying attention to our emotions.

> Ignoring our emotions is turning our back on reality. Listening to our emotions ushers us into reality. And reality is where we meet God. . . . Emotions are the language of the soul. They are the cry that gives the heart a voice. . . . However, we often turn a deaf ear—through emotional denial, distortion, or disengagement. We strain out anything disturbing in order to gain tenuous control of our inner world. We are frightened and ashamed of what leaks into our consciousness. In neglecting our intense emotions, we are false to ourselves and lose a wonderful opportunity to know God. We forget that change comes through brutal honesty and vulnerability before God.[8]

A current point of growth in my own discipleship is learning to recognise my feelings and bring them to God in prayer—realising that "reality is where we meet God." This is about growing in emotional maturity, which is part and parcel of spiritual growth and the journey of discipleship.

I think that the whole burgeoning issue of mental health in today's world prophetically calls us back to the *sanity* of living the Jesus way (Matt 11:28–30). It reminds us that we are all wounded, the journey to wholeness is lifelong, and slow is good.

Is discipleship safe? Is Jesus safe? If by "safe" we mean a Jesus who will never challenge us or ask hard things of us, then No. But if by "safe" we mean a Jesus who will never abandon us and who will lead us in ways that, though sometimes difficult, will help us to flourish until we experience complete wellbeing in the new

---

8. From Allender and Longman, *Cry of the Soul*, 24–25.

creation, then Yes, amen and absolutely. In fact, Jesus himself assures us that he is safe (John 10:9). But it's more than safe. If we are to believe what Jesus says, then this is the mentally healthy way of life God longs us to live.

Slowing down to nurture our relationship with Jesus is pivotal.

In the next chapter, we'll begin looking at how to persevere when things are hard.

THINK. PRAY. DO.

- Have you or a loved one ever experienced issues relating to mental health? What did you learn/are you learning?

- This chapter mentioned the sanity of living the Jesus way. What do you think that entails? And what about the world we live in is so contrary to the flourishing of good mental health?

- Think about any part of your life that could benefit from a slower pace to enable you to experience more of the rest Jesus promises. Take steps towards addressing this and record them in your journal.

PART IV

Battling

Jesus replied, "No one who puts a hand to the plough and looks back is fit for service in the kingdom of God."

—LUKE 9:62

CHAPTERS 9 TO 11 look at three barriers to push through—challenging obstacles and *battles* we face as we follow Jesus.

9

Through Self-Denial and Carrying Your Cross

Then he called the crowd to him along with his disciples and said: "Whoever wants to be my disciple must deny themselves and take up their cross and follow me."

—MARK 8:34

When Christ calls a man, he bids him come and die. It may be a death like that of the first disciples who had to leave home and work to follow him, or it may be a death like Luther's, who had to leave the monastery and go out into the world.

—DIETRICH BONHOEFFER, *THE COST OF DISCIPLESHIP*

THE BEAUTIFULLY ODD COLLECTION of Christians from a variety of churches formed an untidy procession and wound their way around the route through the North London town. It was a racially

PART IV: BATTLING

diverse group, made up of young and old. Most walked in silence and, apart from one or two of the marchers who were chatting and laughing (to the dismay of some), the general mood of the crowd was sombre. It was Good Friday, and some sturdy-looking chap was at the front, apparently quite pleased to be carrying a large wooden cross.

As the group emerged from a side street onto the main road, a double-decker bus rolled past. Loud music was blasting from it and through the windows you could see it was packed with dancing people in all sorts of costumes—Star Wars storm troopers and all. Whoever these people were, they were having a good time. They were, in fact, Jewish people celebrating Purim. Easter and Esther side by side for a brief moment. What a contrast. Two celebrations of deliverance. It looked a lot more fun to be Jewish that day.

Wild celebration and solemn cross-carrying are both valid responses to God's saving work. Large parts of the Western church are, actually, often pretty good at the celebrating bit. But how does cross-carrying work—and is there a place for it outside of that quirky Good Friday reenactment?

Following Jesus can be comforting, satisfying, exhilarating, and feel as if we're "going with the grain of the universe." It can also be mystifying, deeply challenging, countercultural, and counterintuitive. That's because the way of Jesus is an upside-down, right-way-up way of living. It is where we learn that to grow up we must become like a child, the weak are strong, we gain by giving, the humble are lifted up, and leaders are servants—and most of all they are followers.[1] We are *all* followers in the way of the cross.

As disciples, we are learning to deny self and make daily choices to put Jesus and his ways first. We know that the cross is the symbol both of salvation and of discipleship—stemming from the heart of the Triune God who has, from all eternity, lived in mutual self-surrender, and whose love has always in that sense been "cross-shaped" and other-centred. Disciples know that taking up one's cross is a call to embrace the way of God—the crucified life.

1. Matthew 18:3 and 23:12; 2 Corinthians 9:6 and 12:10; 1 Corinthians 11:1.

THROUGH SELF-DENIAL AND CARRYING YOUR CROSS

We know that without our cross we may call ourselves Christians, but it is not Christ we are following.

Everybody in Jesus' time knew what a cross was—that brutal, ugly instrument of tortuous, shameful death. Everyone knew that those who carried their crosses were dead men walking. Yet Jesus thought of the cross as the place of his greatest glory (John 12:23) and he calls every person to the cross-carrying life of self-denial daily (Luke 9:23) and for the rest of their lives. Sometimes people talk (with a saintly look about them) about a cross they feel they "have to bear." We can, then, imagine that only certain unlucky people have that special cross to bear, that most of us can get by as Christians without a cross. But Jesus said the cross of self-denial was for *everyone* who followed him. Every Jesus follower will often face aspects of self that need to be crucified. This is not just for a few poor saints, it's for us all.

This was *not the first thing* that Jesus told his disciples or potential disciples (perhaps because he wanted them to trust in his achievement for *them* rather than their own achievements for *him*). But it was something that he wanted his followers to understand.

Discipleship will call us all to deny ourselves and follow Jesus wherever he leads. Self-denial does not mean that we welcome the abuse others may give us or that we do not try to take good care of ourselves, but it is still costly. It is a direct strike on our human pride, which wants desperately to grant our self everything it wishes.

Self-denial will mean putting Jesus first, and that will mean different things to each of us. But it will involve rejecting or demoting anything that keeps us from giving ourselves completely to Jesus. It starts with understanding that Jesus is Lord.

I began learning about this when I was twenty years old and three years into my relationship with Jesus. I had moved away from home and was living in an apartment. Some small life changes had begun happening. I also started to read my Bible and to pray, eager to develop my relationship with Jesus.

One day I got down on my knees by the bed and spoke to Jesus. "Lord," I began. Then stopped. I'm not sure what happened exactly, but it was as if Jesus stopped me and said, "Hi Tim. Do you know what Lord means?"

It dawned on me that Lord meant something like Master or Boss, so I said, "Lord, I understand! You're in charge of me! From this point on I will go wherever you want me to go, say whatever you want me to say, and be whatever you want me to be!"

How I managed to grow up in a Christian family and be a Christian for three years without knowing the implications of Jesus being Lord is beyond me. But what can I say, except that I'm a slow learner. . . . And I think you'll agree that it was quite a promise I made. It surely has been tested over the years and it's a promise I have not always perfectly kept. Yet the revelation of Christ's Lordship that day has shaped my life profoundly.

Taking up your cross and following the Lord Jesus takes you to places you wouldn't normally go. After some years it took me to the other side of the world. To be honest I felt a little like Jonah must've felt when the fish brought him up and sent him on his way to Nineveh. Landing on the runway in a faraway country, the plane "spewed me up," if you'll forgive the turn of phrase, into a new phase of life overseas. We lived there for some years and came to know a lady I'll call Lydia. Her story demonstrates the courage, cost, and outcome of the cross-shaped life.

Lydia was a strong character and known for her lying, cheating, and manipulating ways. Lydia was a Muslim lady who discovered Jesus through two Muslim-background friends, a married couple.

It happened when she went to stay with the couple in their city. What struck her was the way they seemed different and more alive than ever before. She asked them what had changed to make the difference. They explained how they had discovered Jesus and were now following him as Lord and Saviour. "I want what you've got! Let me have Jesus now!" said Lydia. But the couple could see she didn't really understand what she was asking for, so they told her she was not ready to accept Jesus.

This might sound a bit shocking to some of us, but how often do we declare people Christians on the back of a prayer they've prayed and have hardly understood? It's not surprising that so many may barely think of themselves as Christians, let alone disciples.

Several days into her stay with the couple, now onto her third request to receive Jesus, Lydia explained that she understood that God had sent his Son Jesus to die for her sins on the cross so that she could be forgiven and have eternal life and begin to follow him, that she understood she was eternally lost without Jesus. The couple could see she was genuinely ready and they prayed together as Lydia received Jesus Christ as Lord and Saviour and committed her life to him.

Lydia returned to her hometown and began telling her family members—and there were a lot of them—about Jesus and how they needed him too. But one day, to her surprise, the family elders called her into the front room for a meeting.

Seated around the living room table, the meeting began. The oldest brother spoke on behalf of the whole family. Lydia was to stop talking about Jesus. It was either Jesus or her family. Let her choose.

Through tears, Lydia said she loved them all dearly, but could never choose them over Jesus who had given himself for her on the cross. And with that she was thrown out of the family home and out of town.

Lydia was emotionally devastated and materially destitute. But God is always faithful. He provided a home in a new town and she gradually began to rebuild her life.

As the weeks went by, something strange started happening. One by one, members of her wider family trekked into town to see her. They would stay at her house for a meal, or for a few days, and listen to her as she spoke about Jesus. They were amazed at the new, loving, and truthful person she had become. And one by one many of them came to follow Jesus.

I could tell other stories of courageous cross-carrying as well as some about those who dropped their cross and walked away discouraged by the hardship they faced. The reality is that some press on and some don't.

PART IV: BATTLING

German pastor Dietrich Bonhoeffer famously wrote his book *The Cost of Discipleship* in 1937. During World War II, he was arrested and imprisoned by the Nazis and, just weeks before the end of the war in Europe, was executed by them. His book rightly took aim at the cheap grace or easy-going Christianity of his time. A Christianity he felt was more about following a nationalistic philosophy than a crucified Saviour. Following Jesus is costly and there are always things to leave behind as we carry the cross and follow him.

Here are some of Bonhoeffer's famous words:

> Cheap grace is the grace we bestow on ourselves. Cheap grace is the preaching of forgiveness without requiring repentance, baptism without church discipline, Communion without confession.... Cheap grace is grace without discipleship, grace without the cross, grace without Jesus Christ, living and incarnate. Costly grace is the treasure hidden in the field; for the sake of it a man will gladly go and sell all he has.[2]

Jesus doesn't invite us simply to believe in him and think of ourselves as Christians but not change our lifestyle in any way. His invitation is to the lifelong adventure of discipleship. If you have trusted in Jesus and his finished work for you on the cross—repented and believed—then you are a disciple. Pretty soon he will help you understand that this involves taking up your cross and following him as Lord. Like Lydia, this life of self-denial may involve denying the natural longing for comfort and the loving acceptance of family or friends. Like I experienced, it may involve agreeing with Jesus to go and live in a country that's not on your bucket list (but can become, as it did for me, a home away from home). At other times it may mean denying the urge to have the last word in an argument, fulfil a sexual desire, or hoard possessions rather than share them generously.

What could possibly motivate anyone to take up their cross and follow Jesus? It may surprise us to note that there are selfish reasons for doing so, as well as unselfish ones. By "selfish," I mean

2. Bonhoeffer, *Cost of Discipleship*, 4.

TWO (OR THREE) SELFISH REASONS

First, disciples love to obey and imitate the one they follow. They say, "I desire to do your will, my God; your law is within my heart" (Ps 40:8). They already know that his yoke is easy and his burden is light (Matt 11:30). Desiring/delighting to do God's will doesn't necessarily make it any easier—as Jesus shows us in the Garden of Gethsemane (Matt 26:36–46). But there is a satisfaction in doing God's will that only a disciple can understand.

Second and third, disciples believe Jesus when he says that self-denial is the surprising way of avoiding what we dread and gaining all we ultimately long for: "For whoever wants to save their life will lose it, but whoever loses their life for me and for the gospel *will save it*" (Mark 8:35, emphasis added) or "find it" as Matthew 16:25 puts it.

Today it is common to assert and demand our rights. As those who have been justified, disciples love justice and pursue it on behalf of others. They know that justice delights the heart of God (Jer 9:24) and have heard the call "to act justly and to love mercy and walk humbly with your God" (Mic 6:8). Yet, throughout history, many thousands of disciples have chosen to lay down their own rights and carry their cross all the way to martyrdom because of the supreme worthiness of Jesus, their gratitude for all he has done for them and the joy of the life to come. Many around the world today face mockery, social exclusion, family abandonment, violence, imprisonment, torture, and even death for the sake of Jesus. Chances are that many who read these words won't face much on that list. But it's more than certain that every one of us will face daily challenges to lay down our sin, our pride, our will, our selfish ambitions, our time, our comfort, our politics, our energy, and our resources for Jesus' sake. And as we do, we will find, as Jim Elliot once said (read his story in *Shadow of the Almighty* or *Through Gates of Splendour*), that "he is no fool who gives what he

PART IV: BATTLING

cannot keep, to gain what he cannot lose."[3] Jim and four other missionaries went on to lose their lives in pursuit of taking the gospel to the Huaorani people in the Ecuadorian jungle.

Jim and his colleagues knew that the best really was yet to come, that it was better to carry the cross—come what may—than to live for themselves and ultimately lose everything. They didn't seek death. But they were willing to go where Jesus led them.

But there are also other gains along the way—*this side* of glory.

The apostle Paul writes about a secret he had discovered in the losses he faced as he followed Jesus: as he suffered for Christ, he felt he was somehow sharing in Christ's sufferings. He knew that, through this "fellowship" with his Master, he was becoming more like Jesus and gaining the treasure of a closer relationship with him (Phil 3:4–11).

TWO UNSELFISH REASONS

First, disciples carry the cross of self-denial so that the gospel is furthered. Jesus says, "whoever loses their life for me *and for the gospel*. (Mark 8:35, emphasis added).

We deny ourselves not primarily for ourselves but for the sake of others—for their good. And their ultimate good is to share in eternal life. Jesus is our supreme example of selfless living that benefits others (Phil 2:5–8). Jesus took up his own cross of self-denial for *our* sake. He became a servant for us, so we can become servants of *others* (Mark 10:43–45). Disciples are recognisable by their servant-heartedness (John 13:12–17).

I think back to the formation of a new mission team, one that was to be made up of two existing teams. James, a gifted young South African leader of the English-speaking group, would be the senior leader of the new, larger team. Half of the team was South American, had been living in a different part of the country, and was led, until that time, by Lorenzo. Lorenzo was a vivacious older

3. Elliott, *Shadow of the Almighty*, page 15.

THROUGH SELF-DENIAL AND CARRYING YOUR CROSS

man with a lot of life experience. From a cultural point of view, everyone wondered how Lorenzo would cope by yielding leadership to a much younger man. At the first team meeting, all the questions were answered. Lorenzo and his team members arrived at James' house for the meeting and meal, and everyone greeted each other. The South American folk entered the house and sat down. Lorenzo, however, stayed outside. He rolled up his sleeves, fetched a bucket of water and a sponge and proceeded—with a big smile on his face—to wash James' car. With hardly a word spoken, everyone got the message: *I am your servant. I am denying myself and following Jesus. And I'm happy about that!*

It was the beginning of a special relationship and set the tone for some beautiful years of teamwork. It was a teamwork that saw many lives touched by the gospel.

The second and most important "unselfish" motivation for carrying the cross is the worthiness of Jesus. He says, "whoever loses their life *for me* . . ." (Mark 8:35, emphasis added). This is a key issue for us as disciples. How worthy—how worthwhile—do we think it is, where necessary, to deny self for Jesus? Is he worth it? Is his sacrifice worth it? Is it our goal to bring him pleasure by our wholehearted commitment—to love him as he has so loved us? These are big questions and require some heart-searching.

Whoever wants to be a disciple must deny themselves, take up their cross and follow Jesus. Remarkably, those who lose their lives end up finding them. But the cross comes, as they say, before the crown. This is not, as some might call it, "radical discipleship," it's simply discipleship—the life to which we're called. It will be a core, defining, authenticating mark of our true identity as followers of Jesus.

> Fixing our eyes on Jesus, the pioneer and perfecter of faith. For the joy that was set before him he endured the cross, scorning its shame, and sat down at the right hand of the throne of God. Consider him who endured such opposition from sinners, so that you will not grow weary and lose heart. (Heb 12:1b–3)

PART IV: BATTLING

We can strengthen our ability to carry the cross of self-denial by learning to:

- Enjoy the satisfaction of an obedient life.

- Dread the futility of a self-centred life—remembering that "whoever wants to save their life will lose it."

- Revel in the promise of the cross-carrying life—remembering that "whoever loses their life for me and for the gospel will save it" and that there is *joy set before us.*

- Grow in our conviction of the worthiness of Christ—remembering that Jesus said it is "for me" (see Rev 5:12). A good place to start would be asking the Holy Spirit to open the eyes of our hearts to the beauty, glory, and worth of the One we follow (Eph 1:18–23).

Try for a moment to imagine a world in which everyone practised cross-carrying. . . .

Behind so many of the problems in the world today—whether in relationships, in churches, or between countries—is a failure or refusal to deny self, take up the cross, and follow Jesus.

When the Creator stepped out of his heavenly glory and into his broken world, he travelled the way of the cross. The way of the cross is, still today, the pathway to heavenly glory.

In the next chapter, we'll look at what it takes to press on when life gets harder than we imagined—and what happens when we do.

THINK. PRAY. DO.

- In what ways have you denied yourself and followed Jesus?

- Are there ways that, surprisingly, you have "found" yourself as you have carried your cross?

- How will you need to carry your cross and follow him today?

Through Self-Denial and Carrying Your Cross

- This chapter closed with four ways to strengthen our cross-carrying. Take some steps to addressing the one that speaks most to where you're at right now.

10

Through Pain and Heartache

Yet I will rejoice in the LORD, I will be joyful in God my Saviour.

—HAB 3:18

Good surgeons may have to hurt us but they will not harm us. It is the way they heal us.

—ANONYMOUS

CARRYING THE CROSS OF self-denial is one kind of challenge, but there are other challenges, too. Self-denial is a challenge we choose for *ourselves*; there are some challenges that seem to choose *us*. For this reason, although there are elements of cross-carrying in some of our hardships, we are taking a separate chapter here to explore how following Jesus will involve passing through painful seasons. The headline is that these very times of difficulty become the raw materials for making something beautiful in our lives.

THROUGH PAIN AND HEARTACHE

Mi-sook[1] was a South Korean young woman with a badly disfigured face. She was also a disciple. Mi-sook placed the small pouch into my hands, emptying out the contents as a gift: six or seven variously coloured gems. In broken English she explained to me that what looked now like gems had previously been sharp, jagged pieces of glass. Over time the ocean currents had blown them this way and that in the sand and now they were smooth and beautiful. She had discovered these gems one by one in her walks on the beach.

Mi-sook was conveying to me a precious truth that she had learned the hard way. She told me that she knew that Jesus was using her disfigurement to produce inner beauty.

I'm sure the apostle Paul would have agreed: "Therefore we do not lose heart. Though outwardly we are wasting away, yet inwardly we are being renewed day by day. For our light and momentary troubles are achieving for us an eternal glory that far outweighs them all" (2 Cor 4:16–17).

I have never forgotten that encounter with Mi-sook. That pouch is one of my treasured possessions.

Nor can I forget Steven.

Steven was around forty years old, had cerebral palsy, and lived in sheltered accommodation. He answered the door and I looked down to find him on his hands and knees. At church he used crutches but in his home he found it easier to get around by crawling. As he was recently widowed and new to our church, I was wanting to get to know Steven better. He led me to the living room and we took our seats. Steven thrust a huge Bible into my hands. He used this Bible because his eyesight was failing and he needed the words to be as large as possible. His cerebral palsy made speaking incredibly difficult, but Steven asked me to read Psalm 88 out loud.

I suggest you do that now—it will only take you a couple of minutes or so. Pay special attention to verses 8, 9, and 18, but read or scan through it all.

---

1. Mi-Sook and Steven are pseudonyms, used here for privacy. To preserve anonymity, details have been changed in several other places in this book.

Part IV: Battling

Psalm 88 has to be the darkest psalm in the book.

I read the psalm, looked at Steven, and he was staring into my eyes, nodding.

Silence.

Steven was sharing his bitterness with me. But in a very real way he was also sharing with me his hope. Hope because there was a place in the Bible that described exactly what he was feeling: that maybe somehow, some way, suffering and darkness was not the last word, as it was not for Heman, who found grace to write a psalm that has gone on to speak to countless lives over the millennia.

Is discipleship only for the able-bodied and those who are well? Sadly sometimes that impression may inadvertently be given, but we should remember that, for many, the "logo" of the Christian faith is a disabled man on a cross.

We face, as James puts it, "trials of many kinds" (Jas 1:1). I think of a friend who is same sex attracted but chose the path of celibacy because of their biblical conviction that this pleases God. I think of another friend who is the most dynamic follower of Jesus I know, a great preacher, evangelist, and prayer warrior. In their twenties they anticipated a life spent in active service and global mission but were diagnosed with a degenerative illness. And I think of an elderly friend who found life increasingly difficult after a stroke in their late eighties. Each of these three friends, when faced with a daily battle in a struggle not of their choosing, has chosen to remain stubbornly determined to follow Jesus and to help others know him. And each one has chosen to faithfully follow Jesus despite incredible challenges.

Life can be traumatising. In fact, many of us are so used to living in this broken world that we are numb to how awful it often is—or otherwise have somehow managed, so far, to avoid this reality.

When we know and follow Jesus there will still be dark days. Sometimes we will wonder where God is. We will face many smaller tests and some very big ones, and each one is a key moment for our growth. Some of those days may break us in such a way that

THROUGH PAIN AND HEARTACHE

we never feel the same as before that time—or, like Steven, we may have been born with lifelong challenges that only seem to increase. There are times when we may want to give up. God's promise is that we will never face any of this without him.

Peter tells us that persevering through pain and hardship is part of our calling: "To this you were called, because Christ suffered for you, leaving you an example, that you should follow in his steps" (1 Pet 2:21). This is a hard lesson for our generation here in the West. But I suspect it's never been easy for any generation, anywhere.

On one occasion, the apostle Paul travelled back into an area that he'd had to previously escape after people had tried to murder him. He felt the new believers desperately needed to hear an important message. Luke describes this as strengthening the disciples.

> They preached the gospel in that city and won a large number of disciples. Then they returned to Lystra, Iconium and Antioch, strengthening the disciples and encouraging them to remain true to the faith. "We must go through many hardships to enter the kingdom of God," they said. (Acts 14:21–22)

I look back on many personal experiences of God's hand on and through my life: miraculous provision (1 Kgs 17), healings (1 Cor 12:28), prophecies and words of knowledge received (1 Cor 12:8), as well as empowerments (Acts 1:8), special moments of his Presence and touch (Ps 3:3), and incredible dreams God has given and fulfilled (Acts 2:17).[2]

One of those dreams was quite a story.

Annemarij and I were in Holland visiting family. We woke one morning and both shared about a strange dream we'd had. It was a bit fuzzy but involved turning up late for a performance. It felt like a warning—something to take note of. The strange thing was that we'd *both* had that dream. We wondered if it had been

---

2. If anyone doubts the relevance of the work of the Holy Spirit today, let them read Andrew Wilson's excellent chapter in *Spirit and Sacrament* on the charismata in historical perspective (chapter 5).

PART IV: BATTLING

prompted by something we'd watched on TV the night before or if we'd eaten to much Gouda (Dutch cheese), but we concluded it wasn't that. We talked and prayed but had no idea what the dream could be about and so asked Jesus to make it clear to us.

Some months later, as we were starting to make plans for moving overseas on mission, we had a mission leader visit our home in North London. He spent the day with us and talked about a new team we could join from January 2001. The church where I was ministering had asked us to consider staying longer than planned. However, the mission leader pleaded with us not to be late for the start of the new team. We remembered how God had warned us in the dream, months before, not to be late. We sensed that the timing was right for our move, so we didn't delay. We set off to join the new team and began an extraordinary season of life, seeing God do some very special things.

But there has also been mystery and heartache along the way.

Annemarij and I have been married for nearly twenty-five years. In chapter 8 I mentioned our pregnancy problems. Before we married, we talked like all couples about what sort of a family we'd like to have together. Annemarij wanted five children and I wanted two. So we did a compromise and settled on three. We had a lot of fun choosing names.

We married and soon began trying for our family.

Nothing happened.

For month after month.

Year after year.

Nothing. Happened.

We had every kind of test you could imagine but no cause was found. We pursued various fertility treatments, including three rounds of IVF, but nothing worked.

What do you do when God withholds from you the thing you long for more than anything else? Right there is a big discipleship moment. What are you going to do when your dreams and beliefs are smashed and God doesn't do for you what you know he could?

Several possible responses come to mind:

The "angry-sad" response: We give up and walk away.

THROUGH PAIN AND HEARTACHE

The "lights are on but no one's home" response: Outwardly we project that all is well, whilst inwardly we've parked up our discipleship wagon. We go to church on Sunday, but that's about it.

And there is the "broken but trusting" response: We don't understand but we remember that "in *all* things God works for the good of those who love him, who have been called according to his purpose. For those God foreknew he also predestined to be conformed to the image of his Son" (Rom 8:28–29, emphasis added).

And with the help of the Holy Spirit, we may slowly learn to live and pray in Habakkuk's words (Hab 3:17–18) when we see no signs of God's promised blessings:

> Though the fig-tree does not bud and there are no grapes on the vines, though the olive crop fails and the fields produce no food, though there are no sheep in the sheepfold and no cattle in the stalls, yet I will rejoice in the LORD, I will be joyful in God my Saviour.

Annemarij and I have cried our share of tears, but we have, by God's grace, continued to trust. The logic went like this: "Is God good? Yes. How do we know? Because he gave his only Son to suffer and die for us. Do we understand why we can't have children? No. Can we go on believing that God is good and has our best in mind? Yes, we can."

Getting to that point took time. Grieving and lamenting our loss was not an obstacle or inconvenience to discipleship but part of our learning to live in reality with Jesus as we followed him and he led us through this valley. The heartache changed us. In some ways it grew us. When God does not give us what we think we want most in the world, but we still trust him, we have grown.

But let's back up a moment. Does God really allow—even use—difficulties? Some people struggle with a God who would do this. Two places in the Bible spring to mind.

There is Romans 5:3–5:

> Not only so, but we also glory in our sufferings, because we know that suffering produces perseverance; perseverance, character; and character, hope. And hope does not put us to shame, because God's love has been poured out

PART IV: BATTLING

into our hearts through the Holy Spirit, who has been given to us.

Glorying in our sufferings may seem a bit out of reach—and there will be seasons when that is especially true. But the point is clear. When hard things happen, we know that as we press on and through, we will grow. The promise is that God takes things that could make us despair and turns them into things that will ultimately fill us with hope.

Hope is a special Bible word that refers to our long-term future. Paul is making a direct link between the suffering God allows into our lives and the presence of hope. Not the weak wish for something better that the English word "hope" seems to suggest but the confident expectation of the incredible future we will enjoy together, with Jesus, forever.

God is not like an examiner looking for mistakes but like a parent standing at the edge of the sports field, rooting for our success. As we learn to persevere, our character grows. One of the fruits of its growth is the greater presence of hope. And, wonderfully, hope in turn helps us in our suffering. I have lost track of how many times I have seen the power of this hope to strengthen followers of Jesus in our church through their most gut-wrenching times.

God is so committed to our long-term good—to our Christlikeness—that he will use anything to achieve it. This is not a "nice" truth but it is a good one and true, nevertheless. Our part is to learn to press on and keep trusting. And perseverance is possible because of the presence of the Holy Spirit, who works in us what we simply couldn't do on our own.

Then there is Hebrews 12:4–13:

> In your struggle against sin, you have not yet resisted to the point of shedding your blood. And have you completely forgotten this word of encouragement that addresses you as a father addresses his son? It says,
>
>> "My son, do not make light of the Lord's discipline,
>> and do not lose heart when he rebukes you,
>> because the Lord disciplines the one he loves,
>> and he chastens everyone he accepts as his son."

Through Pain and Heartache

> Endure hardship as discipline; God is treating you as his children. For what children are not disciplined by their father? If you are not disciplined—and everyone undergoes discipline—then you are not legitimate, not true sons and daughters at all. Moreover, we have all had human fathers who disciplined us and we respected them for it. How much more should we submit to the Father of spirits and live! They disciplined us for a little while as they thought best; but God disciplines us for our good, in order that we may share in his holiness. No discipline seems pleasant at the time, but painful. Later on, however, it produces a harvest of righteousness and peace for those who have been trained by it. Therefore, strengthen your feeble arms and weak knees. "Make level paths for your feet," so that the lame may not be disabled, but rather healed.

Just as good parents discipline and train their children, so the Lord chastens us. The idea of discipline in this passage is less about punishment and more related to what we could call "strength training" (Heb 12:12).[3] The Lord is helping us to become stronger and more fruitful.

This is a difficult truth for some. God doesn't bubble wrap us. He loves us far too much for that. His plans for us stretch beyond giving us an easy today into an unimaginably perfect eternity.

I know that hardship has softened my heart and made me more able to empathise with others, that my relationship with God is stronger because I'm more convinced than ever that the sunshine of his love is still shining, even when the dark clouds of life are obscuring it. At a deeper level, many disciples have discovered the insight that in the darkest moments, when God seems most absent, he is actually most present. There was no darker moment, nor greater Presence, than when God, in Jesus, hung on the cross. And many have experienced that the most excruciating times of their lives have yielded the richest treasures of encounter and intimacy with God.

---

3. See the note relating to this passage (Hebrews 12:4–13) on page 2200 of *The Renovaré Spiritual Formation Bible*.

Part IV: Battling

Let me underline that matter-of-fact little phrase from the Hebrews 12 passage: *"no discipline seems pleasant at the time, but painful."* It will hurt. And we may at times feel that God has not kept his promise to not give us too much to handle (1 Cor 10:13). Trite answers to those going through hardship are really not helpful. But neither is it helpful to deny the reality taught in scripture that God grows, strengthens, and refines us through these difficulties (see also 1 Pet 1:6–7). And so we don't lose heart. And importantly, every time we grow, we gain fresh strength and capacity to face future storms.

When life is hard, we need to honestly face, lament, and grieve our pain or sense of loss. With God's help we get back on our feet, trusting, following, and stronger.

The next chapter looks at one more type of challenge that comes our way: What to do when our discipleship and disciple-making is marked by as many groans and blunders as it is signs and wonders.

THINK. PRAY. DO.

- Take an honest look at the way hardship or heartbreak has affected your journey of discipleship. Pay special attention to how it has moved you forward, brought you to a standstill, or even sent you backward. What do you see?

- Read Psalm 13 and write your own prayer of lament using the same kind of structure.

- Ask Jesus who he has placed in your life to share this journey with—and perhaps also the lament you have written.

11

Through Failure and Slow Growth

The third time he said to him, "Simon son of John, do you love me?" Peter was hurt because Jesus asked him the third time, "Do you love me?" He said, "Lord, you know all things; you know that I love you." Jesus said, "Feed my sheep."

—JOHN 21:17

I'm talking about discipline and perseverance. And all cute little comments aside . . . there comes a point in every race—it could be the fifth mile, it could be the twenty-fifth—but, eventually, you're gonna hit . . . what runners like to call "the wall." And when you do . . . you won't be able to breathe or think or even move. All you're gonna wanna do is give up. And I have a very strong feeling . . . that that's exactly what you're gonna do, Dennis.

—FROM THE MOVIE *RUN FATBOY RUN*

Part IV: Battling

I REMEMBER THE DAY that I passed my driving test. I was seventeen years old. The poker-faced examiner turned to me and said, "Well, Mr Sutton . . ." [deliberately pausing]—and my heart sank—"I am pleased to tell you that you have passed your driving test." Joy and relief. The first thing I did when I got home was rip off my L plates. Not a learner anymore—a real driver . . . or so I thought.

There is no ripping off the L plates—or the D plates—for you and me. We are disciples until heaven, because discipleship is not a programme or course that you do—it's a whole-life apprenticeship to Jesus. Perhaps remembering that will help keep us from discouragement. If we're honest, we still get some pretty basic things wrong. We can fall out with others; we are tempted to be proud, greedy, lustful, and lazy; we gossip and are fearful and ungracious; we can be prayerless, over-busy, and misguided. We all fall short on the ABC of discipleship, which is to learn to love God with all that we are and our neighbours as ourselves (Matt 22:37–40).

George Verwer (1938–2023) was an enormously influential Christian leader. He founded the mission organisation Operation Mobilisation, which has touched literally millions of lives around the world. George was passionate, honest, and funny. By the grace and power of God, George sustained a humble, godly witness to the very end of his life. He was also famously honest about his failures and temptations. In this, George was a huge encouragement to countless people as he lived the grace and truth of God.

Repentance isn't a single decision but a choice we need to make over and again—to change our minds, to turn our hearts, lives, bodies around to Jesus. And we need to know that crashing out in sin and failure, though messy, painful, and saddening the heart of the Father, need not be the end of our story.

Sadly, some seem to feel it's their duty to keep others in their place—that those who have fallen or failed in the past have no hope of playing any significant part in the life of the community going forward. This is a shame in the truest sense. Churches must be places of redemption and restoration. Church discipline must be carried out in some cases. Certain roles may not be appropriate anymore. But church discipline is never simply punitive, it aims

THROUGH FAILURE AND SLOW GROWTH

for the restoration of the one who has sinned (2 Cor 2:6–8). Wise love and careful discipline are needed and this will take time.

All kinds of people are disciples. There's no one type of character more likely to follow him. There's a place for each of us, with all our character strengths and flaws.

The first twelve are listed in Mark 3:13–19. From the Gospel stories we know more about some of them than others. We know that Simon, James, John, Andrew, and Philip were fishermen. And we know that Peter was impulsive and James and John could be hot-headed. Matthew was a tax collector when he met Jesus—a breed known and hated in those times for their creative accounting and own-pocket-lining tendencies. Simon the Zealot was probably a militant. Thomas was famously a sceptic. Bartholomew was also initially sceptical. And Judas was greedy. It's interesting how Mark's list starts with Simon Peter, who famously let Jesus down in his moment of greatest need and denied even knowing Jesus, and ends with Judas Iscariot, who betrays Jesus for cash. So it's really clear that when he makes the important choice of his first followers, Jesus doesn't go for perfect people.

Sometimes people hold back from following Jesus because they think they have to be good enough. Jesus actually said that we need to be, in a sense, bad—or perhaps desperate—enough. "Jesus said to them, 'It is not the healthy who need a doctor, but those who are ill. I have not come to call the righteous, but sinners'" (Mark 2:17). We come as we are, with all our brokenness and faults. He just asks us to follow, trust, and obey him. And he even helps us to do that.

Twice in these verses, here in Mark 3, Jesus renames them. Simon is called Peter or Rock—and as Jesus changes and grows him he becomes something of a rock in God's church. And James and John are called Sons of Thunder and we know from the story that they were hot-headed boys. Perhaps by calling them by this name, Jesus was humorously calling attention to a part of their life that needed transforming through the Spirit. Their passion would be less harmful to others and put instead to good use for the Kingdom of God. Disciples are always open to what it is that Jesus

PART IV: BATTLING

needs to change in us as we follow him, spend time with him, and are sent out in his name.

The disciples' journey of change was not straightforward. Fast forward to the night that Jesus was betrayed. The disciples are having Communion and, shall we say, all heaven is not breaking loose (Luke 22). Jesus starts talking about how one of them will betray him. Their denials lead to an argument about who is the greatest among them. Jesus announces Peter's impending failure and Peter denies it. And the holy meal finishes with them so misunderstanding the way of Jesus that they think they are pleasing him by taking up arms (Luke 22:38). Three of them head out with him for the most poignant pre-Crucifixion moment in Jesus' life, and instead of supporting him they fall asleep. When the arresting party arrives, every one of them runs and leaves him alone—except for a moment Peter, who ends up chopping off the ear of a poor civil servant, presumably after aiming for his neck.

Someone might say, "Well this was before Pentecost and the coming of the Spirit." After Pentecost we do see the difference the help of the Holy Spirit makes—Peter, for example, regains faith and grows in wisdom and boldness. But as we read through the book of Acts we see there are still complaints, moral failures, cultural misunderstandings, disagreements, disciples not making the cut, Christian leaders divided. Except in the sad case of Annanias and Saphira (Acts 5:1–11), most of these incidents are not fatal. But the point is, as anyone with half a conscience knows, that we all mess up sometimes. This is not a permit to give up and peel off the D plate. It is rather a reminder that if Jesus chose people like that to start the whole thing, then there is hope for us too.

Nobel Prize winner Daniel Kahneman (1934–2024) was a well-known Israeli American psychologist and economist. He spent decades exploring the psychology of judgement and decision-making and talks about this in his bestseller, *Thinking, Fast and Slow*. In the book he focuses a lot on our thinking and how biased we are as humans—and the mistakes we tend to make.

THROUGH FAILURE AND SLOW GROWTH

What can be done to overcome these problems? After many decades of painstaking scientific work, this is Kahneman's conclusion:

> The short answer is that little can be achieved without a considerable investment of effort. . . . [M]y intuitive thinking is just as prone to overconfidence, extreme predictions . . . as it was before I made a study of these issues. I have improved only in my ability to recognize situations in which errors are likely. . . . I have made more progress in recognizing the errors of others than my own.[1]

How refreshing to hear someone admit that they are biased and that they see other's problems more clearly than their own. And whether he knows it or not, Daniel Kahneman has hit the nail on the head. Spiritually, there is little we can do on our own. Yet as Jesus-followers we are not pessimistic and we are not alone. On the contrary. We know that we have the Holy Spirit working from within and the promise of Jesus never to leave us. We may fail and fail often, others may fail us, but Jesus won't—nor will he give up on us (Heb 13:5b).

It is so important not to let discouragements and personal failure paralyse our discipleship. We confess and repent where needed. If necessary, we try to sort out the mess we have made. Then we get back up and on the journey with Jesus. We live in grace (Eph 2:10).

Failure comes in all shapes and sizes—moral failure, relationship failure, professional failure (where we mess up in our work). I remember running a workshop for English teachers one time when we lived overseas. We filled a college auditorium with gifted teaching professionals. As the "expert" foreigner, native speaker, and trained and qualified English teacher, I gave a presentation to demonstrate a clever new teaching technique. I was quite proud of myself, until someone pointed out that my grammatical construction (scribbled on the white board) was completely wrong. Imagine. A local teacher with a less than perfect English accent

---

1. Kahneman, *Thinking, Fast and Slow*, 417.

125

PART IV: BATTLING

correcting me, the English "expert". . . in front of a room full of people. FAIL. Red face. The shame of it! But I feel a little better just by sharing this with you.

Failure is actually quite popular at the moment. Some years ago in Mexico, five friends spent the evening together. These young professionals discovered that they had never shared their stories of failure with one another—only their successes. So they decided to host an event in which people could talk openly about the things they'd got wrong. They would give several entrepreneurs seven minutes to share their blunderful tales using ten images—after which there would be time for questions and answers. They gave the events a rude name which doesn't leave much to the imagination but communicated the general idea. The concept took off and went global, with hundreds of people attending in two hundred cities in at least seventy-five nations. The founders say that these events lead to greater resilience and the important factor of learning from mistakes.[2] There's a lot of laughter and something of the sting of failure is taken away.

What if we did more of this in our gatherings? I'm certain it would be encouraging to a lot of us. We would realise that we were not the only ones who blow it. And those who share their stories may be released from the sense of shame and empowered to turn their worst moments into learning points. And, importantly, we would laugh more.

Some failures are of course no laughing matter. Relationship failure is a particularly painful case in point. Over the years, Annemarij and I have been privileged to come alongside a number of married couples experiencing difficulties—some but not all of whom we have been able to help. At these times we draw from the early days of our own married life when there were genuine struggles. For us, the presence of a mature and loving couple coming alongside made all the difference. And that is my suggestion for any who are reading these words and going through something similar. Get a couple you can trust to spend some weeks

---

2. Birrane, "Yes, You Should Tell."

THROUGH FAILURE AND SLOW GROWTH

and months walking together with you both. If that's not possible, there will be some good Christian counsellors who can be of help.

Failure impacts us in different ways. It knocks some of us down and we struggle to get back up, feeling unworthy. For others—perfectionists, especially—the fear of failure can prevent us from stepping out and trying new things. Which one of these are you most likely to be?

If there has been serious *moral* failure or if we find ourselves stuck in some kind of persistent sin, then we need to get help from others. Ask a Christian leader or another trusted and mature believer to pray with you. Talking about this kind of failure is still crucial. In John 20:23 the risen Jesus confers on the disciples the authority to forgive sins. And in James 5:16, in the context of prayer for healing, we read, "Therefore confess your sins to each other and pray for each other so that you may be healed." We need to take these two scriptures more seriously and find ways of honestly sharing our failures with those who can listen and pray with us as we confess. We don't need to do this in a special confession booth in a church building, though I am not necessarily against the practice. Whilst we can confess our sins in private, there is something powerful about doing it with other people. "If we confess our sins, he is faithful and just and will forgive us our sins and purify us from all unrighteousness" (1 John 1:9).

We find others to travel with us. We learn to be patient with ourselves. Weeds grow quickly, but strong, tall trees take time. We remember that every one of us has something to give and there is no one alive who can make exactly the contribution we can, to the flourishing of God's kingdom. So we make sure to be part of a Bible-believing, Jesus-loving church; to join with others in learning how to follow Jesus; to have daily times alone with him. And we remember that wherever we are right now and however we feel we're doing, Jesus' promise *to us* is that "surely I am with you always, even to the end of the age" (Matt 28:20). So we never, ever give up. We learn from our mistakes—they show our weaknesses and blind spots. But we don't give up. We are loved. There is grace. We learn *that* and pass it on to others.

PART IV: BATTLING

In the final chapter, we will look at the remarkable task that Jesus gave us—and some practical ways to go about it.

THINK. PRAY. DO.

- What mistakes have you made and who have you shared about them with?

- Have you ever felt like giving up on following Jesus? What was the cause of that? What has kept you going?

- Who might need your encouragement in their discipleship?

- With a trusted disciple friend or in a prayer triplet, plan for a brutally honest time of sharing your unvarnished failures together. Afterwards pray about them together.

PART V

Birthing/Begetting

"Don't be afraid; from now on you will fish for people."

—LUKE 5:10B

CHAPTER 12 LOOKS AT the task of discipleship, which is to make more disciples—*birthing* new generations of those who follow Jesus.

12

Discipling Disciples

Then Jesus came to them and said, "All authority in heaven and on earth has been given to me. Therefore go and make disciples of all nations, baptising them in the name of the Father and of the Son and of the Holy Spirit, and teaching them to obey everything I have commanded you. And surely I am with you always, to the very end of the age."

—Matt 28:18–20

Whether we are called to serve God by working as a tax inspector, an artist, a social worker, a home-maker or a preacher, God calls us to go out of the confines of the church to make disciples in his world. That can be in media or academia, in suburbia or Siberia, on the stage or using the pages of a book.

—Krish Kandiah, *Dysciples*

Reproduction. That's our task as disciples.

PART V: BIRTHING/BEGETTING

Matthew has been working his way up to this point. The Great Commission sums up so many of the themes Matthew has been teaching in his Gospel and brings them to their natural conclusion. But over the years we have come to the point where we can over-emphasise the Great Commission as a missionary text and under-emphasise it as a discipleship text. Let me unpack that a bit for us.

Growing up in a missionary home, I thought the Great Commission meant everyone should pack their bags and go to the other side of the world to preach the gospel. There is no getting away from the fact that the thrust of Matthew 28:16–20 is missionary and it is global. But mission is bigger than evangelism and discipleship. And we get our biblical basis of mission from the whole Bible, not just from a few verses in the New Testament.

Chris Wright's definition is my favourite. He writes that mission is "our committed participation as God's people, at God's invitation and command, in God's own mission within the history of God's world for the redemption of God's creation."[1] That's a hefty statement. Wright goes on to show that the whole Bible is the unfolding story of God's mission. God is at work to redeem his broken creation (Col 1:16). His mission is much larger than a plan to simply get people into heaven, central though that is. Mission may start in the transformed hearts and lives of individuals, but it doesn't end there. It aims at the transformation of everything.

The trouble with thinking of these verses mainly as a "missionary" text is that we can end up with a narrow view of mission *and* we feel we can keep the Great Commission at arm's length. All the action is "over there"—far from our own quite "normal" lives and reality.

In these five short verses, Matthew is not trying to provide us with a general motivation for mission. He wants us, specifically, to get out there and make disciples—not simply converts—starting wherever we happen to be. With this one command, say Greek language scholars, comes three participles and three ways of carrying it out: *going*, *baptising*, and *teaching*. This envisages a discipleship

1. Wright, *Mission of God's People*, 23.

132

DISCIPLING DISCIPLES

community of Abrahamic ilk—"Go" (see Gen 12:1–3). It is a community obediently on the move with one clear task.

This is also a vision of discipleship that calls to mind images of ordinary believers moving through their everyday lives and rubbing shoulders with all sorts of people—*going* along through life and sharing the love of Jesus on their frontlines, the places where they live and work.

Is that what the church looks like today, or has it turned into something else? Something like a group of people coming to a holy building on a holy day to hear a holy man speak and to sing holy songs—then Monday to Saturday going back to living life in the "real world."

This relative lack of active disciple-making is known as "the great omission" in the Great Commission. Why the omission? We looked at various possible reasons in chapter 2—the myths that surround this whole subject. Later in this chapter we will look at some practical ways any of us can make sure we're personally not omitting the Great Commission.

The Great Commission is so central to our thinking on discipleship and disciple-making that we need to walk slowly through it together. Only then will we think about some ways to get involved in discipling others.

From the beginning . . .

THEN THE ELEVEN DISCIPLES WENT TO GALILEE, TO THE MOUNTAIN WHERE JESUS HAD TOLD THEM TO GO. WHEN THEY SAW HIM, THEY WORSHIPPED HIM; BUT SOME DOUBTED. (MATT 28:16–17)

For a passage that contains one of the most amazing promises ever made, it's not a very promising start. Only eleven disciples—one is missing. We know who. And they are a bunch of worshipping doubters. Of course they are—it's been a crazy, heartbreaking, mind-bending few days and they can't process it all. And they never had quite got it (Luke 24:44–49). How many doubted? Two

PART V: BIRTHING/BEGETTING

or three? Four or five? And when the eleven heard the scale of the task given them, what did they think? "All nations—us? Really?!?!"

I love the impossibility and honesty of the Great Commission. It grounds what follows in the reality of human frailty. We doubt and we worship. We feel there are not many of us and there is a big, broken world out there. This is all sounding quite familiar.

"ALL AUTHORITY IN HEAVEN AND ON EARTH HAS BEEN GIVEN TO ME." (MATT 28:18)

Do we sometimes wonder what right we've got to disciple others? Who am I to assume such a position as disciple-maker? Isn't that a bit proud of me? Doesn't it imply I'm somehow more advanced than others? When I began discipling others, I felt these questions keenly and needed the encouragement of Christian leaders to remind me of the urgency and legitimacy of this task.

The authority of Jesus is the basis of our disciple-making. It is an authority in heaven, meaning he has power over the heavenly realms, over angels and demons (see Eph 1:18–23). And it is an authority on earth. Jesus has shown this awesome authority by stopping raging seas with a word, by healing broken bodies with a touch, by forgiving sins. He astounded crowds with his teaching. "You have heard that it was said . . . but I tell you . . ." (see Matt 5). He taught as one who had authority—taking people to the heart of God's word.

The authority Jesus describes here is the same authority Daniel saw in a vision (Dan 7). Daniel saw a heavenly being who was given everlasting authority over all nations on earth. People of every nation were worshipping him. Jesus is saying here that Daniel's prophecy has started to come true.

After the resurrection, as Jesus meets his dazed disciples, he orders them—with an authority that surpasses anything anyone has ever known—to go out and spread his Kingdom rule. This all-encompassing authority is the basis of disciples' ability, as God leads, to heal the sick and expel demons. (Note that in the book of

DISCIPLING DISCIPLES

Acts it's not only the apostles who ministered healing and deliverance—see Acts 6:8 and 8:6–8.)

This authority is the basis of our authority, with bold humility, to communicate the claims of the kingdom of God on peoples' lives. What right have we? No right of our own. But the full authority—the authorisation—of Jesus.

"THEREFORE GO AND MAKE DISCIPLES OF ALL NATIONS . . ." (MATT 28:19)

In Daniel's vision the Son of Man received the worship of all nations. But as Jesus stands in front of his disciples, that vision is still a long way from fulfilment. Even today, billions of people are unreached and undiscipled. The nations Jesus has in mind are not nations or countries as we think of them today. They are ethnic or people groups.

Our vision must be global. We can never be content to concentrate our disciple-making efforts on our own little area. Jesus clearly wants the community of disciples to think big, to allow ourselves to feel out of our depth and staggered by the scale of the task he has given us. Perhaps only that will drive us to desperate, urgent prayer.

In our disciple-making we need to cross borders and boundaries—cultural, class, racial, national, political, ethnic, and comfort boundaries. We try to be aware of the boundaries that separate us from others—and then cross them. We ask the Holy Spirit to help us become culturally flexible, like the apostle Paul: "I have become all things to all people so that by all possible means I might save some" (1 Cor 9:22b; see 1 Cor 9:19–23). We learn to be more concerned that our church gatherings reflect the culture of God's kingdom than our own culturally bound traditions.

Serious followers of Jesus ask themselves what they can personally do to see the nations becoming disciples. They will use their prayers, resources, and whatever opportunities come their way to see the global goal of the Great Commission fulfilled. Churches will prayerfully consider strategic ways of partnering with other

PART V: BIRTHING/BEGETTING

churches, indigenous workers, and organisations with the same heart to see disciples made and churches planted. In these times of unprecedented global challenges, they will strive to see what God is doing, and join in. How many of us think through the part we have to play in blessing the nations or ask Jesus if he wants us to relocate for this purpose?

". . . BAPTISING THEM IN THE NAME OF THE FATHER AND OF THE SON AND OF THE HOLY SPIRIT . . ." (MATT 28:19)

Jesus reminds us here that we are trinitarian disciples. We want to see people coming to know the gloriously mysterious God who is Three-in-One and One-in-Three—and publicly declaring that faith in baptismal waters. And through baptism we are immersed into the life and mission of our Triune God. This is why we can pray as Jesus teaches: *Our* Father in Heaven. . . . He is now, amazingly, our Father too.

In John 5:19, Jesus says: "Very truly I tell you, the Son can do nothing by himself; he can do only what he sees his Father doing, because whatever the Father does the Son also does." Former archbishop of Canterbury Rowan Williams makes an insightful comment on this:

> The heart of discipleship is bound up with the life of the Trinity; as we develop our understanding of the trinitarian life of God, uncovered for us in those wonderful passages of John's Gospel, so we develop in our understanding of what provides the root and energy of our being disciples here and now. We see and we do, not just because that is the way that discipleship or studentship worked in the ancient world; we see and do because that is what the Father and the Son are involved in for all eternity.[2]

2. Former archbishop of Canterbury Rowan Williams makes this astute observation on page 15 of *Being Disciples*.

When we are disciples and making disciples, we are doing something deeply trinitarian.

". . . AND TEACHING THEM TO OBEY EVERYTHING I HAVE COMMANDED YOU." (MATT 28:20)

We are baptised into a new way of life—obediently following the way of Jesus. What is the way of Jesus? Think, for example, of what he taught his disciples in the Sermon on the Mount (Matt 5–7). These chapters are essential study material for anyone wanting to take their discipleship seriously. In living out the Sermon's principles, we build a solid house before the storms come (Matt 7:25).

Around 60 percent of the four Gospels is about the life and teachings of Jesus, so there is plenty of food for thought and action. We can go through Matthew's Gospel and find that Jesus' first three commands (after the call to follow him) are to rejoice and be glad if we are persecuted for his sake, to let our lights shine, and not to think Jesus came to get rid of the Old Testament (Matt 5:12, 5:16–17). And as we study the Gospels, we see that there is a lifetime of learning for us as disciples—to love enemies, to seek God's glory and purposes above everything else, to not worry, to not judge others, and to be ready for the future return (the second coming) of Jesus. Jesus is saying, I want you to teach them obedience in all these things. Not simply to be good Christians and know these things and to be able to quote chapter and verse but to practise them. "Blessed rather are those who hear the word of God and obey it," as he once said (Luke 11:28).

And according to the Bible, *inability* to teach others the way of Christ can be a sign of immaturity (Heb 5:12).

PART V: BIRTHING/BEGETTING

"AND SURELY I AM WITH YOU ALWAYS, EVEN TO THE VERY END OF THE AGE." (MATT 28:20)

This promise reminds us of his name (Matt 1:23): Emmanuel, God with us. Jesus is saying here: "You're right to think that the task of discipling the nations is impossible! Without me *it is*. But you don't have to do it without me. I'm with you in this. My presence and power to guide and help you. Always." *I am always with you* is a disciple-maker's promise. We always remember that we do it not simply *for* him but *with* him. And this is the main reason we don't crumple up in a heap under the enormous weight of the Great Commission.

A final thought on this before we turn to suggestions for putting the Great Commission into practice.

Just notice something God says in Isaiah. In Acts 1:8 we see Jesus using this same phrase to send his followers out to proclaim, to witness to his Kingly rule over all the earth. As part of that witness, we call others to be disciples of Jesus.

> "You are my witnesses," declares the LORD, "and my servant whom I have chosen, so that you may know and believe me and understand that I am he." (Isa 43:10a)

In its original context, this Isaiah verse is of course referring to Israel. It is the "so that" bit which is interesting to us. Very often we think of witness, evangelism, and disciple-making as *so that* others may come to know Jesus. But God says here that he has chosen Israel to be a witness *so that* they may know, believe, and understand him. This is clearly suggesting that when we serve God's purposes we come to a deeper understanding and experience of God himself. One commentator puts it like this: "The purpose of witness is not just to convince the world but also to confirm the faith of the witnesses."[3]

Many disciples have discovered over the years that there are things that we ourselves can only learn by active engagement in disciple-making. Not only does it help others to come to life with

3. Webb, *Message of Isaiah*, 176n54.

DISCIPLING DISCIPLES

God, but it is an essential part of our own journey of discipleship. We can see this in the experience of the seventy-two disciples, who returned from a short mission trip having learned crucial lessons about the power and authority of God and also about their identity and security (Luke 10:17–20).

Today the church continues to grow, particularly in the global South. But with well over a billion people to be born within the next decade, the need for serious global disciple-making remains. In the UK, the results of the 2021 census showed that for the first time in more than a millennium, a minority of the population claim the Christian faith as their own.

What is the answer? What has always been Jesus' answer?

"Make disciples."

If there were no other reason to do this, we should do it because it works. The church only spread throughout the earth because disciples made disciples.

The world feels more divided, volatile, lost, and broken than ever. But we aren't pessimistic. Disciples believe that the way of Jesus leads to healed lives, loving relationships, justice, peace, reconciliation, and environmental renewal—as well as to a restored relationship with God and eternal joy. We live in the light of God's loving intentions for his creation (Isa 66:22; Rom 8:18–25; 2 Pet 3:13; Rev 22:1–5). If we are to take scripture seriously, then we understand that without Jesus, people are "without hope and without God in the world" (Eph 2:12). And so we take seriously the call of Jesus to make disciples of the nations in our time—to be people who will help others to experience the goodness of the Lord in the land of the living (Ps 27:13). The big question, of course, is *how*?

Here are five answers, or approaches, to that question.

1. DISCIPLE YOURSELF

We take seriously the need to spiritually look after ourselves— like David in 1 Samuel 30:6b, who "found strength in the LORD his God."

PART V: BIRTHING/BEGETTING

We commit to becoming an apprentice of Jesus. If our faith has been shallow, revolving solely around going to church on Sundays, we resolve to walk more closely with Jesus from now on—in our weekdays and workplaces, at study, home, or play.

2. DISCIPLE YOUR FAMILY

Some of us have little disciples just waiting for our input. Yet there are Christians who won't get their children reading the Bible or teach them about Jesus. They feel they don't want to "force" their beliefs on their children, that their children must make their own young minds up or that somehow they can outsource spiritual formation to their church's children's ministry. The trouble is that if *we* don't teach our kids, then the world around us *will*. It is our task to tell them about Jesus, to introduce them to the Bible, to help them love church, to show the difference God makes in our lives, and to pray earnestly for them. When they are old enough, they can make their own choices, but it's not a choice when all they have is one side of the story, a side that will be loud and clear to them from the world around. It is a devastating dereliction of duty to leave our children at the mercy of the shifting sands of culture, with its broken value systems and falsehoods.

Moses teaches the people of Israel:

> Hear, O Israel: the LORD our God, the LORD is one. Love the LORD your God with all your heart and with all your soul and with all your strength. These commandments that I give you today are to be on your hearts. Impress them on your children. Talk about them when you sit at home and when you walk along the road, when you lie down and when you get up. Tie them as symbols on your hands and bind them on your foreheads. Write them on the door-frames of your houses and on your gates. (Deut 6:4–9)

The people of God were to disciple their children.

What can we learn from Moses about discipling our families?

DISCIPLING DISCIPLES

- Make it personal: "On your hearts." If it's not on *your* heart, why should it be on anyone else's?

- Make it integral: "With all your heart and with all your soul and with all your strength." Every part of you is involved.

- Make it memorable: "Impress them on your children."

- Make it verbal: "Talk about them."

- Make it normal: "When you sit at home and when you walk along the road, when you lie down and when you get up."

- Make it visible: "Tie them as symbols on your hands and bind them on your foreheads. Write them on the door-frames of your houses and on your gates."

- Make it fun: I just added that, but you know it's true!

Looking back, I realise how blessed I was to have godly parents who read the scriptures to me each day before school and prayed with and for me, who motivated me to read the Bible and modelled love, hospitality, and humility.

Those of us blessed to be parents, grandparents, godparents, aunties, or uncles find the most obvious, memorable, creative, and doable ways to talk about Jesus with our families. A friend of ours regularly looks after his grandchild. His son is not a Christian. But from the very beginning, this grandparent has been gently speaking Jesus into that little life. We sow into our families' lives. Some of us are, perhaps, heartbroken because we have not seen our kids develop and grow into disciples themselves and they may even seem a million miles from that ever happening. But the story isn't over yet.

And to be clear: this isn't all just about adults making disciples of children. Children need to be given opportunities to reach out and disciple others. Teens reaching other teens is a powerful thing. Jesus set about changing the world through his "youth group." Gavin and Anne Calver make this point strongly in their excellent book *Unleashed*: "Jesus' twelve disciples were certainly young, almost all under the age of eighteen and some even as young as fifteen."[4] Part of discipling people is teaching them how to disciple others.

4. Calver and Calver, *Unleashed*, xxii.

PART V: BIRTHING/BEGETTING

The strength of this all-age family approach is that it roots disciple-making in the everyday world of nappies, family squabbles, taxiing the kids around, and washing the dishes.

3. DISCIPLE EACH OTHER

As has been said more than once, we each need to be in a small group, triplet, or prayer partnership. Believing spouses can hopefully see in each other a partner in discipleship and disciple-making. But married people still need to be meeting others for mutual spiritual growth and input.

The primary way in which most of us today will be discipled may be by mutual disciple-making. This is where we understand that *as we walk closely with each other we can walk closely with Jesus.* We are the body of Christ. We recognise that we need more than to "go to church" on a Sunday. We can come and go to church for years without walking far down the path of discipleship.

Remember the following scriptures?

"And Saul's son Jonathan went to David at Horesh and helped him to find strength in God" (1 Sam 23:16). This is what we need to regularly do for each other.

"And let us consider how we may spur one another on towards love and good deeds, not giving up meeting together, as some are in the habit of doing, but encouraging one another—and all the more as you see the Day approaching" (Heb 10:24–25).

Small groups work best when they eat, share about their daily lives, pray, and study the Bible together. But they go up another level when their genuine focus is not simply pastoral but discipleship.

A small group can become a discipleship group when it regularly asks members questions that help draw out implementation intentions, like "What is Jesus teaching me right now, what am I going to do about it and when?" These questions and discussions are followed up briefly the next time the group meets. This kind of gentle accountability is powerful if it can be carefully developed and wisely practised.

DISCIPLING DISCIPLES

Remember, you're joining this group to help disciple others, not simply as a consumer of what the group can offer you.

As we have said before, if small groups aren't possible or are just not for us, then we can ask two trusted Christian friends if they are up for forming a triplet—for meeting regularly to share coffee and life, to pray and learn from Jesus together. Or failing that, we look for just one person to partner with in prayer and discipleship. And as we set up these arrangements, it can often help to get our expectations clear and make things less formidable: we perhaps agree to try the triplet or prayer partnership for six to twelve months and review it after that time. This gives us an easy get-out clause if for whatever reason the meetups aren't working. Try to set timings up and keep to them: will you meet for an hour once a week or once a month? For an hour or two hours? Will you meet at a café, in your home, or for a walk? How deep will your sharing go? What are the expectations regarding confidentiality? Setting clear guidelines at the start helps to make these meetings more fruitful.

Practise mutual disciple-making.

The strength of this approach is that it relies heavily on a primary resource that God has created for our spiritual progress: the Body of Christ.

4. DISCIPLE THOSE AROUND YOU

Making disciples means we look around. We take every opportunity for sharing our faith with those with whom we come into contact. And proclaiming Jesus to those around us requires both our actions and our words. Words without actions can be cold, hard, and empty. Actions without words can be misleading. People may never ask or wonder why you are like you are.

It's important that every disciple has their personal salvation story ready—written down, sharpened up, and salient points memorised. (Without wanting to sound morbid, your written testimony can be a powerful witness at your funeral, as recently happened in our church in the life celebration for my friend Gerry.)

PART V: BIRTHING/BEGETTING

With our story ready, we pray often for openings. At the very least, this will increase our spiritual sensitivity. Remember that the quality of person we are and the quality of the work we do (and the way we do it) will speak volumes and be remembered. We ask people questions about their lives and what they believe. We read books on how to engage with the questions or objections people may have. We practise answering those questions with our friends from church. We remember that we're a link in the chain and the task is, at the very least, to leave those with whom we rub shoulders at least one step closer to Jesus.

Some of us will feel confident enough to take some steps towards more intentional, regular discipling of those we know. But honestly speaking, many of us find sharing our faith with others daunting and the most experienced of us don't get it right every time. Perhaps we need to remember that it's good to reach out *to* others *with* others. The individualistic spirit of the Western world can blind us to the opportunities we have to share our outreach. In recent decades, "missional communities" have grown in popularity—disciples sharing life together on mission, making evangelism more human, organic, sustainable, and actually even enjoyable! Some groups gather for movie nights, others for meals. There is no end of ways to form attractive groups through which we aim to make new disciples.

Operating on our own as singles or as couples/families, we can offer the hospitality of a coffee or a meal, at home or in a café or (if you can afford it) restaurant. Food has been at the heart of disciple-making from the beginning (John 21:12; Acts 2:46). Eating together breaks down barriers and opens hearts. A simple but sincere welcome, with a drink or bite to eat, can sometimes be more effective than a big meal, with the formality that can creep in with that.

5. CHRISTIAN LEADERS DISCIPLE OTHERS

"You then, my son, be strong in the grace that is in Christ Jesus. And the things you have heard me say in the presence of many

DISCIPLING DISCIPLES

witnesses entrust to reliable people who will also be qualified to teach others." (2 Tim 2:1–2)

In some circles it used to be said that leaders should look for FAT (Faithful. Available. Teachable) people to disciple. There may be some wisdom in that, if we are thinking of good material for Christian leadership. After all, an unfaithful, unreliable, and un-teachable trainee pastor, elder, youth leader, or missionary is not very promising! Although no one should be ruled out. Some of us don't start out very promising! And as we saw in the last chapter, Jesus clearly didn't choose the nicest and most perfect people to be his first followers.

In reality, Christian leaders need to try to disciple as many people as possible. Yet if Jesus only managed twelve full time, and out of the twelve he seemed to focus on three, then we should cer-tainly start small.

Pastor and people should see Sundays as part of discipleship training—listening carefully for a word to embrace and inspire our walk with Jesus. We can also see the times before and after the service as opportunities to lovingly serve one another.

Leaders and those longer in the faith have the crucial task of raising up other leaders, as Paul says to Timothy in the passage above. As a pastor myself, can I lovingly say to my colleagues that I believe we should not only be thinking of our own preaching and teaching ministry but also looking out for new people God is gifting. We should be in investing in the next generation of pastors and preachers and passing on skills. For some years I have run periodic preaching classes, which include opportunities to preach. Likewise, deacons or elders can be thinking about who they can help train up or invest in, perhaps in their area of ministry respon-sibility. Youth workers, musicians, welcomers, you name it . . . dit-to. Too often when a need arises, we look for ready-made solutions. The answer is to be proactive now, in preparation for the future.

If Christian leaders made it a normal part of their role to gather a small number together for a season of special discipleship input, I believe there would be huge results. People often benefit so much from the weeks, months, or years we invest in them, and some of them will go on to disciple others. This is a huge challenge for pastors, who are run off their feet with all the tasks they are usually expected to carry. So it will require wise and courageous use of time and very likely saying "no" to other things on the to do list. Conversations about this with our co-leaders and churches are important. Any disciple who is serious about following Jesus will be trying to disciple others. But Christian leaders should be leading the way in this.

Those entrusted with running Baptism, Confirmation, or faith-exploring classes should make sure to include teaching in these sessions on the life of discipleship. If you are not a leader in church, you can still be part of the culture change. You could, for example, graciously tell your leaders that you don't simply wish to be cared for by them pastorally but would love to be enabled and equipped by them to follow Jesus more fruitfully.

The strength of this fifth approach is that Christian leaders, in theory, have a firm grasp of the faith.

What if all five above-mentioned approaches were part of our normal Christian lives? Whether we are from a house church or high church, they are all possible. Wouldn't it be great if we took the time to work out clear and workable ways to help these things happen?

Jesus aimed to make disciples who made disciples. When Jesus called us to follow him, he had in mind a way for you and me to fulfil this calling and bear fruit. We need to accept and own this task. We need to ask the Holy Spirit to lead us into the most authentic way of expressing this calling, with the unique lives, experiences, gifts, characters, families, life stages and circumstances that we have. The way you make disciples will be different to the way I do it.

BEING SUBVERSIVE LIKE JESUS

How can we reach people and get through the barriers we feel they have put up? If we look at how Jesus did it, we see that he was subversive, probing and penetrating spiritual body armour through

DISCIPLING DISCIPLES

the powerful spiritual "weapons" of parable and prayer. He captured people's hearts and minds before they realised what was happening. So pack your bags and get ready. Take your questions and your listening; take your helping and your hospitality; take your stories, vulnerability, and prayers. Take your love. And go.

> I'm telling you to open your eyes and take a good look at what's right in front of you. These . . . fields are ripe. It's harvest time! (John 14:35 MSG)

Look around to see who you can invest in. It could be those still on a journey but far from faith in Jesus. It could be that you find yourself a little further down the road of discipleship than a person who would value your loving input. It could be that your best opportunities to disciple others will come as you prayerfully prepare and position yourself to give, to disciple, whenever you can—on the move. Look around and see who Jesus has put there.

Look again at the five parts of this book. Understand that if you can grasp something of the calling, goal, power, challenge, and task of discipleship, then you are ready to help others to do the same. You don't need to wait to be perfect before you step out to make disciples. Use the lessons taught in this book and try to share them with others. And you will find that Jesus is with you, just as he promised.

THINK. PRAY. DO.

- In what way(s) are you already involved in discipling others?
- Talk with Jesus about ways of discipling others that you find most natural or enjoyable, and which ones are more challenging for you.
- In your journal, write a list of those you can invest in and pray regularly over it. Be open to the opportunities every day and make disciples!

Conclusion

CONGRATULATIONS ON MAKING IT to the end of this book! I pray that it has helped equip you to steadily move further into life with Jesus.

You are a believer, a child of God, a Christian—but what if you always thought of yourself primarily as a *disciple*? And when people asked you about your faith, what if you called yourself *a follower of Jesus*, because that's what you are?

If you have read this book alone, perhaps now is the time to re-read it with a friend or friends, to discuss the *Think. Pray. Do.* suggestions at the end of the chapters.

I want to leave you with two short stories and a challenge that paints in black and white the choice we face.

I was in a big auditorium at an international Christian event.

Up on the stage, the mime artist was talented and very funny. He mimicked being in church as the offering plate came along the aisles. He gingerly—perhaps slightly reluctantly—took out his wallet and put a coin on the plate. The attendant didn't move. The plate was still there in front of him. Nervously, he got his wallet out again and put a note on the plate. The attendant still didn't move. So this time the churchgoer got a handful of notes and placed them all on the plate. The attendant did not move on. It started to get a bit silly. The churchgoer was now sweating as he placed his whole wallet on the offering plate. Still no good. So, he took off his watch, the shirt off his back, his shoes, his trousers, and handed

148

CONCLUSION

them over. . . . All to no avail. Finally, he got it. He took the offering plate, placed it in front of him, stepped into it, and offered the whole of himself.

> Therefore, I urge you, brothers and sisters, in view of God's mercy, to offer your bodies as a living sacrifice, holy and pleasing to God—this is your true and proper worship. (Rom 12:1)

I've known the famous old hymn that sings about deciding to follow Jesus and not turning back all my life. But I somehow only recently discovered the poignant backstory. It vividly demonstrates what a living sacrifice can look like.

In the mid-nineteenth century, an Indian man and his family came to faith in Jesus. The authorities demanded that they recant their faith. Simon K. Marak and his entire family did not, and they were executed.

Some say that, as he stood before the accusers, Simon spontaneously composed and sang the words of the song. Others say that the evangelist Sadhu Sundar Singh composed the song, based on Simon's words to his killers. Either way, behind the words is a powerful true story of a family that made a choice.

We too have a choice. Will God get our spare change or all of us? Life is rarely black and white. But when it comes to discipleship, we're either following Jesus or we're not.

Deciding to follow Jesus is not only about a single, crucial choice. It will mean making many decisions day by day, week by week.

This book has tried to address the scandal of discipleship-free Christianity and claimed that following Jesus authentically means:

- a real *Beginning* of the journey with Jesus,
- an active commitment to *Becoming* like Jesus,
- quality time spent *Being* with Jesus,
- *Battling* through hardships with and for Jesus,
- and being part of the *Birthing* of new followers of Jesus.

CONCLUSION

Writing about discipleship has made me more keenly aware than ever of how much I still need to grow more like Jesus. But 1 John 3:2 encourages me that, though I am far from where I should and even could be, a day is coming when my transformation will be complete: "Dear friends, now we are children of God, and what we will be has not yet been made known. But we know that when Christ appears, we shall be like him, for we shall see him as he is."

So don't hold back! With the help of the Holy Spirit, give yourself wholly to Jesus and follow him. For "Christ loved us and gave himself up for us" (Eph 5:2). And as the old disciple-maker once put it, he "died for all, that those who live should no longer live for themselves but for him who died for them and was raised again" (2 Cor 5:15).

Epilogue

MOVING THROUGH THE LAND

THE TOWNSFOLK MOVED STEADILY through the Gate, ushered eagerly along by the Gardener-cum-Guide.

Hearts full of the adventure set before them, in they went, spreading out throughout the land.

They travelled light with the Guide close at hand, a map, and—once through the Gate—none travelled alone.

The topography of the land meant that the way was harder for some. There was laughter and tears in the valleys and plains.

From a vantage point, it was clear that this multitude of travellers were slowly making their way to the same destination. And everyone seemed to know that the greatest of all *joys* lay ahead.

—

The Gate is Jesus.
The townsfolk are us.
The land is discipleship.
The Guide is the Holy Spirit.
The map is the Bible.
The destination is eternal joy and uninterrupted union with God.

EPILOGUE

People who live this way make it plain that they are looking for their true home. If they were homesick for the old country, they could have gone back any time they wanted. But they were after a far better country than that—heaven country. You can see why God is so proud of them, and has a City waiting for them.

—(HEB 11:14–16, MSG)

Appendix

PATHWAYS to Understanding the Bible

MANY OF US HAVE heard people apparently rejecting the Bible because "anyone can make it say whatever they want." On the one hand that *is* of course true—people do twist the Bible. On the other hand, there is such a thing as a *right* and a *wrong* way to interpret the Bible (see, for example, Neh 8:8 and 2 Tim 2:15). So in that sense, we clearly may *not* make the Bible say whatever we want.

If we want to understand the Bible, we first need to come with *faith and humility*, believing that the Bible is what is says it is—written by people but fully inspired by God: "All Scripture is God-breathed and is useful for teaching, rebuking, correcting and training in righteousness" (2 Tim 3:16). As we read the Bible, just as the apostles needed the Holy Spirit's help to understand it, so we ask him to help us (John 14:26; Eph 1:17–18).

If the whole Bible has authority to direct our lives, the next step is to seek to understand its message to us, and that is sometimes not a straightforward thing. But since the resurrection of Jesus two thousand years ago, there have been a number of *widely accepted, tried, and tested ways* of approaching the Bible rightly.

PATHWAYS TO UNDERSTANDING THE BIBLE

Some passages of scripture are naturally harder to understand than others. But as we apply the following methods, we will by God's grace get to the meaning of the passage in question.

Try the acronym PATHWAYS:

P is for Plain meaning: What is the plain meaning of this passage? So often the meaning is plain and understandable and we don't need to make things more complicated. But sometimes we will need to think about the other parts of this acronym.

A is for Author's intention: What did the original human author mean by this? The ground rule here is "a text can never mean something that it never originally meant."

T is for Type of literature: Is it poetry, parable, letter, or prophecy? A parable isn't "historical fact." Jesus did not say it is necessary to believe in a literal prodigal son! His story was making a wider point. We can ask the question: Is this passage descriptive or prescriptive (describing how something was, or telling us what to do)? Knowing what type or genre this literature is will help us in understanding the meaning.

H is for Historical interpretation: How has this passage or theme been understood by the church throughout the ages? Sometimes we can forget that the Holy Spirit has been around for a long time and has been helping God's people to understand scripture all that time. The church hasn't always got it right and there is always new light to come from God's Word. But we should think and pray very long and hard before taking a major turn on a long-established interpretation of scripture.

Some people have questions about the Old Testament laws. Many Protestant theologians have accepted the ancient "threefold division of the law" as being a great way to understand how it applies to Christians today. They identify that the Old Testament law comprises, first, *national* laws for Israel as a nation—and these laws do not apply to Christians, although as part of God's Word we may still learn important principles from them. Then there are *ceremonial* laws, which were for Israel's system of worship—and since Christ has fulfilled these laws by being the crucified and risen "Lamb of God who takes away the sin of the world," these

PATHWAYS TO UNDERSTANDING THE BIBLE

laws no longer apply to us, though again we may learn from them. Finally, there are the *moral* laws, the Ten Commandments and others, which still stand today and apply to us all. So, some but not all of the three types of laws will be *God's laws for us*; but all of the laws remain *God's Word to us*.

W is for What contexts: What is the historical, social, political situation it was written to or about? Knowing this will help us understand the original meaning and therefore what the text may be saying today. And also ask (rather than take an isolated verse as the final word) what is the wider biblical context? What do other parts of the Bible say? The Bible is often the best interpreter of the Bible!

A is for ABC: How does the actual language of this passage help you to understand its meaning? Paying attention to the grammar, vocabulary, style, structure, thematic organization, and imagery can help us to delve deeper into the meaning of a given text. Are certain words repeated? Or is a literary device being used, such as a chiastic structure, where the central meaning is located in the centre of a paragraph rather than at the beginning or end?

Y is for Your bias: As you read this passage, what has your upbringing or culture "programmed" you to think about it? It may help to try to think ourselves into other's shoes—how they may receive the text. It's good to take a self-critical step back like this.

S is for Son of God, Saviour: Last but not least, how does this passage point to Jesus and the gospel and help us to know, follow, and treasure him? Jesus says the whole Bible is about him (Luke 24:25–27, 24:44–47; John 5:39) and leads us to salvation through faith in him (2 Tim 3:15).

NOTES

Why not take a verse or passage of scripture with which you struggle and apply some or all of the above steps—and see where you end up!

PATHWAYS to Understanding the Bible

Having a good study Bible is the minimum for anyone who wants to really understand the Bible. Bible commentaries like The Bible Speaks Today series or Tom Wright's New Testament for Everyone series are also invaluable.

Recommended Reading List

THE FOLLOWING BOOKS, IN whole or part, have been especially helpful to me.

The Cost of Discipleship, Dietrich Bonhoeffer

Life Together, Dietrich Bonhoeffer

Atomic Habits, James Clear

The Bible and Mental Health, Christopher C. H. Cook, Isabelle Hamley, eds.

Discipleship, Peter Maiden

The Message of Discipleship, Peter Morden

Disciple, Juan Carlos Ortiz

The Jesus Way, Eugene Peterson

Emotionally Healthy Discipleship, Pete Scazzero

Discipleship, David Watson

Following the Master, Michael J. Wilkins

The Great Omission, Dallas Willard

Being Disciples, Rowan Williams

Bibliography

Allender, Dr. Dan B., and Dr. Tremper Longman III. *Cry of the Soul: How Our Emotions Reveal Our Deepest Questions About God*. Colorado Springs: NavPress, 1994.

Bailey, Kenneth E. *Jesus through Middle Eastern Eyes*. London: SPCK, 2008.

Barth, Karl. "To clasp the hands in prayer is the beginning of an uprising against the disorder of the world." Quote found on Bible Portal. Accessed August 19, 2023. https://bibleportal.com/bible-quote/to-clasp-the-hands-in-prayer-is-the-beginning-of-an-uprising-against-the-disorder-of-the-world.

Birrane, Alison. "Yes, You Should Tell Everyone About Your Failures." BBC, March 13, 2017. https://www.bbc.com/worklife/article/20170312-yes-you-should-tell-everyone-about-your-failures.

Bonhoeffer, Dietrich. *The Cost of Discipleship*. London: SCM, 2015.

Bono. *Surrender: 40 Songs, One Story*. London: Hutchinson Heinemann, 2022.

Bridges, Jerry. *The Gospel for Real Life: Turn to the Liberating Power of the Cross . . . Every Day*. Colorado Springs: NavPress, 2002.

"British Telecom 'Beattie Ology' TV Ad 50 Sec Advert." Video. YouTube, Accessed January 23, 2024. https://www.youtube.com/watch?v=jC_-r-J69qA.

Calver, Gavin, and Anne Calver. *Unleashed*. London: Inter-Varsity, 2020.

Clear, James. *Atomic Habits*. London: Cornerstone, 2018.

Cook, Christopher C. H. "What Did Jesus Have to Say About Mental Health? The Sermon on the Mount." In *The Bible and Mental Health: Towards a Biblical Theology of Mental Health*, edited by Christopher C. H. Cook and Isabelle Hamley, 128–40. London: SCM, 2020.

Definitions. S.v. "audient." Accessed August 7, 2023. https://www.definitions.net/definition/audient.

Elliott, Elisabeth. *Shadow of the Almighty: The Life and Testament of Jim Elliott*. London: Hodder and Stoughton, 1959.

Evangelical Alliance. *Time for Discipleship? 21st Century Evangelicals*. Spring 2014. https://www.eauk.org/church/resources/snapshot/time-for-discipleship.cfm.

BIBLIOGRAPHY

Friesen, James G., et al. *Living from the Heart Jesus Gave You*. East Peoria, IL: Shepherd's House, 1999.

Harris, Alex and Chrissy Remsberg. *On This Rock: Simple Lessons and Achievable Habits for Church Growth*. Self-published. UK: Firestarters Network, 2023.

Ishiguro, Kazuo. *Klara and the Sun*. London: Faber and Faber, 2021.

Jackson, Debbie. "'One Person Turned Up to Watch My Fringe Show.'" BBC, August 8, 2022. https://www.bbc.com/news/uk-scotland-edinburgh-east-fife-62464032.

Jolley, Matt. "What Is a Whole-life Disciple?" *What Will You Discover Today? Culture and Discipleship—Research and Development* (blog). London Institute for Contemporary Christianity. Accessed September 9, 2023. https://licc.org.uk/resources/what-is-a-whole-life-disciple/.

Kahneman, Daniel. *Thinking, Fast and Slow*. London: Penguin, 2011.

Kandiah, Krish. *Dysciples: Why I Fall Asleep When I Pray, and Twelve Other Discipleship Dysfunctions*. Milton Keynes: Authentic Media, 2009.

Keller, Tim. *The Reason for God: Belief in an Age of Scepticism*. London: Hodder and Stoughton, 2009.

———. "Why Catechesis Now?" The Gospel Coalition, October 10, 2012, Christian Living. https://www.thegospelcoalition.org/article/why-catechesis-now/.

Lewis, C. S. *The Screwtape Letters*. London: HarperCollins, 2002.

Life Application Study Bible. New International Version. Wheaton, IL: Tyndale, 1988.

Maiden, Peter. *Discipleship*. Milton Keynes, UK: Keswick Ministries and Authentic Media, 2007).

Manning, Brennan. *Abba's Child: The Cry of the Heart for Intimate Belonging*. Colorado Springs: NavPress, 1994.

McGrath, Alister. *Making Sense of the Cross*. Leicester: Inter-Varsity, 1992.

Milliken, David. "Depression and Anxiety Drive Increase in UK People Too Ill to Work." Reuters, July 26, 2023, United Kingdom. https://www.reuters.com/world/uk/depression-anxiety-drive-increase-uk-people-too-ill-work-2023-27-26/.

Morden, Peter. *The Message of Discipleship*. London: Inter-Varsity, 2018.

Ortiz, Juan Carlos. *Disciple*. London: Lakeland, 1976.

Peterson, Eugene H. *The Jesus Way: A Conversation on the Ways that Jesus Is the Way*. Grand Rapids, MI: Eerdmans, 2011.

———. "Living into God's Story." Missionworldview.com, Unpublished Resources. Accessed January 23, 2024. https://missionworldview.com.

The Renovaré Spiritual Formation Bible. San Francisco: HarperSanFrancisco, 2005.

Scazzero, Peter. *Emotionally Healthy Discipleship*. Grand Rapids, MI: Zondervan Reflective, 2021.

Simons, Daniel, and Christopher Chabris. "Selective Attention Test." Video. YouTube, March 10, 2010. https://www.youtube.com/watch?v=vJG698U2Mvo.

BIBLIOGRAPHY

Stott, John. *The Cross of Christ*. Nottingham: Inter-Varsity, 1986.

———. "John Stott's Final Sermon: The Model—Becoming More Like Christ." *Christian Today*, August 17, 2007. https://www.christiantoday.com/article/john.stott.final.sermon.the.model.becoming.more.like.christ/12442.htm.

Thorne, Helen, and Dr. Steve Midgley. *Mental Health and Your Church: A Handbook for Biblical Care*. N.p.: Good Book Company, 2023.

Wardle, Terry. *Strong Winds and Crashing Waves: Meeting Jesus in the Memories of Traumatic Events*. Abilene, TX: Leafwood/ACU, 2014.

Watson, David. *Discipleship*. London: Hodder and Stoughton, 1981.

Webb, Barry. *The Message of Isaiah*. Leicester: Inter-Varsity, 1996.

Wilkins, Michael J. *Following the Master*. Grand Rapids, MI: Zondervan, 1992.

Willard, Dallas. *The Great Omission*. Oxford: Monarch, 2006.

Williams, Rowan. *Being Disciples: Essentials of the Christian Life*. London: SPCK, 2016.

Wilson, Andrew. *Spirit and Sacrament: An Invitation to Eucharismatic Worship*. Grand Rapids, MI: Zondervan, 2018.

Wright, Christopher J. H. *The Mission of God's People*. Grand Rapids, MI: Zondervan, 2010.

Wright, Tom. *Mark for Everyone*. London: SPCK, 2001.

Milton Keynes UK
Ingram Content Group UK Ltd.
UKHW051005160724
445380UK00008B/80